IT'S A MENTAL THING!

IT'S A MENTAL THING!

5 Keys to Improving Performance & Enjoying Sport

GREGORY A. DALE, PhD
JAMIE E. ROBBINS, PhD

Excellence in Performance
Durham, North Carolina

ISBN 978-0-615-35597-9

Design and production by Chris Crochetière,
BW&A Books, Inc., Durham, North Carolina

Images courtesy of Duke University Sports Information,
Gary Petit, Mark Hergan, and Winston-Salem State
University Media Relations.

Dedication

I would like to dedicate this book to Cammie, Abbey, Graham, Jacob and Luke for their willingness to let me have time to write. All of you have been so supportive throughout the process. I hope this book will serve as a guide and inspiration to my children as they pursue their paths in life.

[GREG DALE]

I would like to dedicate this book to Aunt Joyce. Although she lost her own battle, I hope and believe her experience will encourage her family to look outside themselves, inside themselves and to one another to find the purpose, the challenge and the fun in every day.

[JAMIE ROBBINS]

Contents

Foreword

I have to admit that after reading other "motivational" books, I had my skepticism about anyone attempting to jump into this genre. I was always left with a feeling that the author just didn't completely grasp what high level athletics and competition were ultimately about. I can say, however, without reservation, that I was impressed by Greg and Jamie's work. It was the first book that I have read in a while that had me thinking "Yes! I can totally relate to the words on these pages." Kudos, this is not an easy task. After reading the book, I reflected on the way I approached basketball. I looked at the way I prepared, handled my triumphs, and managed my fears. Even after playing 9 years in the NBA, I found myself realizing there is the great potential for growth and improvement in basketball and it involves the 6 inches "between the ears." I would hope that any athlete looking for an edge on their competition would read this book and realize that what separates the good from the great, the winners from the also-rans is not quickness, agility, strength or anything to do with athletic prowess but rather the ability for the individual athlete to maximize their inner ability to motivate, handle pressure situations, and focus. I believe this book tackles each of these points concisely and gives the athlete the tools to achieve this mental edge.

[SHANE BATTIER]
Professional Basketball Player, Houston Rockets
National Basketball Association All-Rookie Team
National Basketball Association All-Defensive Team

Acknowledgments

I want to sincerely thank all of the coaches, athletes and colleagues who provided valuable feedback on the manuscript. A special thanks to Don James and Shayna McGeehan for your diligence in the review process. All of you have provided insights that will surely make this book more meaningful for those who read it.

[GREG DALE]

I want to thank the coaches, athletes, and my colleagues who helped throughout the writing process. Specifically, I want to thank my dad for his insights and suggestions and Daan for always supporting me and giving me my space when I was in the zone (unless he was bored).

[JAMIE ROBBINS]

Introduction

How much of your sport success is "a mental thing?" Most athletes believe their sport is anywhere from 50–90% mental. More importantly most athletes also admit to devoting only 5–10% of their training to their mental game. This is an obvious paradox and not ideal if the mental side of sport is truly so important. What about you? Do you train your mind with the same level of commitment you train your body? Do you work on your psychological skills with as much intensity as you practice your physical skills? Do you possess the mental skills needed to help you improve your performance and enjoy the daily challenges of your sport?

Athletes from Michael Jordan to Lance Armstrong have touted the importance of commitment, confidence, desire and the ability to work through obstacles in achieving success. Others have explained how enjoying the challenge is critical to staying active and productive in sport. Sport commentators are constantly discussing how an athlete's mind influences his or her performance. And, the commands "be confident," "focus" or "relax" are heard in every athletic venue. Therefore, the importance of these mental skills on athletic performance is not in question. The only question is whether you are willing and committed enough to work on these skills. Willie Mays, a Hall of Fame baseball player, is quoted as saying, "It isn't hard to be good from time to time in sports. What is tough is being good every day." Being a good athlete from time to time requires talent. Being a great athlete every day requires a lot more. You may have the talent to be good today, but do you have the talent, commitment, confidence, poise under pressure, and character needed to be even better tomorrow?

Think about it! How does a high school swimmer erase a poor performance from his mind quickly enough to swim well in his second race moments later? How does a collegiate volleyball player stay focused on her athletic performance after a heart-breaking loss in her family? And, how does a senior on the football team stay motivated to work hard day after day when he never gets a chance to compete in the games? How can athletes learn to control their thoughts, rather than allowing their thoughts to control them? What do athletes need to maximize their physical talent? What influences the outcome between two athletes who possess the same physical skills and physical attributes? All of these questions can be answered with one phrase: "It's a mental thing."

Our intention in writing this book is to help you develop or improve your mental skills to not only help you perform better, but also enjoy the process. We want you to be able to excel under tough circumstances, focus with distractions, and find your personal motivation to keep going each day. Most importantly, we want you to understand that you control your mind. Your mind does not control you. These lessons also are applicable to individuals performing in other venues such as business professionals, students, dancers or musicians. Although our examples focus primarily on team and individual sport athletes, we hope you will adapt them to improve performances in any and all areas of your life.

Throughout the book we will provide examples, suggestions and strategies based on our experiences as former athletes and coaches, and our current roles as mental training coaches working with athletes from middle school through the professional and Olympic ranks. Think of this as your introduction into mental training. Take your time in identifying mental skills you already possess and skills you need to improve. Keep in mind, just as it took you years to learn and improve the physical skills, it will take you time to hone your mental skills as well.

The following chapters are focused on the five factors we believe are essential for any athlete to be successful. Chapter one discusses the importance of committing to your sport. The chapter highlights the importance of setting goals and engaging in quality practice habits while still maintaining a healthy balance in your life. The second chapter focuses on how you can become a more confident athlete by using strategies and engaging in behaviors focused on what you can do as opposed to what you cannot. Chapter three explains the importance of appropriately interpreting and handling pressure in sports. The focus is on recognizing your current responses and modifying them to empower rather than break you. The fourth chapter discusses how positive character can influence you, your team and your performance. This chapter demonstrates how your manner of handling minor or major adversity reflects your character. Finally, chapter five discusses enjoying the journey. We explain the importance of maintaining your passion throughout your athletic career. There are other topics that could have been included, but we believe these are the five keys to improving your athletic performance and enjoying sport. Throughout all of the chapters you will notice the reoccurring themes pertaining to (a) altering your interpretation, (b) changing your responses, and (c) focusing on the process. To successfully make these changes, you will need to recognize your current thoughts and behaviors and make modifications based on our suggestions. We aim to provide both directions and guidance to help you walk away with a more advanced mental game.

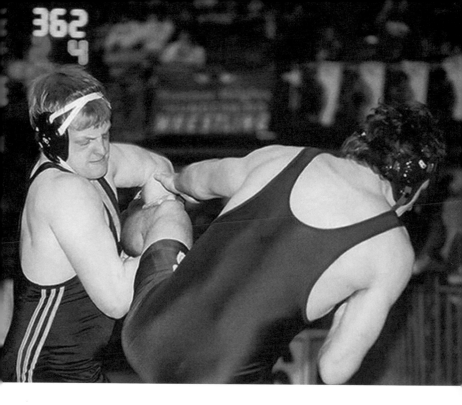

Commitment: Walk the Talk

The vision of a champion is bent over, drenched in sweat, at the point of exhaustion, when nobody else is looking.
MIA HAMM

I know the price of success: dedication, hard work, and an unremitting devotion to the things you want to see happen.
FRANK LLOYD WRIGHT

Think About It

Take a moment to begin examining your commitment level by answering the following questions:

Do you have an unwavering determination to succeed?

Do you take pride in everything you do as an athlete?

Do you set quality goals that help you achieve success?

Do you have a purpose for practice each day?

Are you easily distracted by outside factors during practice?

Do you have a healthy balance between your sport and life?

Truly committed athletes share qualities and behaviors that set them apart from the rest. Therefore, should you desire to join those ranks and reach your full potential, you must:

- Develop an unwavering determination and deep sense of pride
- Set appropriate goals
- Develop quality practice habits
- Maintain a healthy balance

Develop an Unwavering Determination and Deep Sense of Pride

Great athletes have an incredible determination to succeed. They know what they want and relentlessly pursue their goals. These athletes do not need others to motivate them to wake up early or train extra while others are sleeping. Instead, they set two alarms if necessary and they find a way to get in the extra time. Truly committed athletes ask coaches to come early or stay late to help them improve skills and techniques. These individuals can be seen practicing on their own day and night. They are the consummate "gym rats" because they know that talent alone is not going to take them where they want to go.

This attitude and desire was evident in one highly recruited college basketball player. Although he already was earning a great deal of playing time and knew his position on the team was solid, he still made time to work on his shooting when everyone else was home relaxing. At 10:00 at night he would sneak into the gym and work on his jump shot. His coach did not tell him to do this. No other athletes on his team had done this before him. He made the extra effort because he was committed to becoming the best basketball player he could be. This athlete went on to be one of the leading scorers on his college team, a critical athlete to the success of that program, and he currently is playing in the National Basketball Association.

Great athletes also demonstrate a deep sense of pride in everything they do. They complete workouts with the purpose of improving or helping a teammate as opposed to just getting them done. These athletes care about the effort exerted, not just the outcome. They demonstrate displeasure with mediocre performance when they know they could have done better, while showing satisfaction on days when they did everything they could. Just like the student who writes and re-writes a paper before turning it in, athletes with pride are not satisfied with just completing a task, instead they want to know they did their best work. This attitude is obvious to teachers, coaches, and teammates, who recognize these individuals by their attention to detail, refusal to cut corners, and willingness to push hard when the task is tough. These are the first athletes on the field and the last to leave. They are the athletes setting up a pick-up game in the off-season or working on stick skills before practice. These athletes set themselves apart from everyone else. They are very coachable and coaches love working with them.

A high school soccer player was told during pre-season that her position was being changed from back to midfield. She had played defense for three years and starting her senior year in a new position seemed a difficult task. This athlete asked her coach for game tapes from the previous year so she could study the position more completely. She wrote down questions at night and brought them to her coach in the morning to ensure she understood and could be productive in her new role. This athlete was not willing to under-perform that season just because her position changed. On the contrary, she took pride in herself and her team and ended up truly enjoying the season.

The concepts of determination and pride appear first because we believe they are the foundation for everything else discussed in the following pages. If you are determined and take pride in being an athlete, you likely will take suggestions from this book seriously and implement the strategies provided. If you are not determined or lack pride, you likely will read them, admit they would be helpful, but not add them to your regular routine. Our hope is you are reading this book because you are determined and because you do take pride in your performance, and more importantly, you are willing to make changes to improve.

Set Appropriate Goals

The general population often talks about goal-setting. Unfortunately most self-reported goals turn out to be unfulfilled "New Year's resolutions." Whereas the general population is less effective in their goal setting endeavors, the overwhelming percentage of truly successful athletes do set goals and create plans to actually achieve them. Goals are significant because they provide direction and a sense of purpose for action. They serve as reminders for why you train early, late or long, and why you are out in the wind, rain, snow and sun. They help answer the question, "Why am I doing this?" If you already set goals, you are on the right track. If not, now is the time to start.

Before beginning this practice, it is important to understand the difference between outcome, performance and process goals. Many athletes only set outcome goals. Examples include, "Make All-State or All-American," "Win a conference championship," "Go 10–0 during the regular season," "Start every game," or "Be voted 'best work ethic' at the end of season." These goals can provide a sense of direction but alone they are not good enough because they are not completely within your control. Think about it. You can work very hard every day and have what you believe is statistically a great season and still not be chosen as an All-American or All-Conference selection. Additionally, you can play your best but still lose a game or competition. And, while you can influence it, you certainly do not have control over your playing time or the award your coach gives you at the end of the season. The outcome goal provides a direction but no specific and controllable actions to get you there.

Therefore, for every outcome goal, you should have at least a couple of performance and process goals to help you succeed. Performance goals are more within your control because they are typically measured against your previous performances. Examples of performance goals include, "Increase first service percentage in tennis from 75 to 95%" or "Improve number of offensive rebounds in basketball from eight to ten." Again, these are all great ideas, but without a plan to make that improvement, you will not see many changes. This is where process goals become important. Process goals allow you to delineate exactly what you must do each day or on a given skill to reach the outcome or performance goals you desire. Examples include "hit 40 field hockey balls before practice each day," "run five extra sprints at the end of practice twice a week," or "write down a purpose before practice each day." In other words, the process goals are the daily plan. The table on page 11 helps illustrate how to link process, performance and outcome goals.

To reiterate, once you set outcome goals, it is important to shift the focus back to performance and process goals. We encourage athletes to focus the majority of their attention on process goals. These are most effective because they allow athletes to measure and rate their improvements each day because these goals are specific, measureable, and action oriented.

If you are not yet sold on the importance of process goals, think about rock climbers. Have you ever seen climbers on sheer cliffs with little or no safety equipment, literally hanging by their fingernails and toenails? These individuals are clearly focused on the next hand or foothold. When they begin the

Outcome	Performance	Process
All-state as a wide receiver in football	Catch every ball that is thrown my way during each game	Run ten extra passing routes after each practice
Win a championship in golf	Improve the number of fairways hit from 12 to 15	Follow my pre-shot routine for every shot during the round
All-conference point guard in basketball	Improve assist to turnover ratio from 3 to 1 to 5 to 1	Practice dribbling drills for twenty minutes, three days a week after practice
Start every game in volleyball	Increase my serving percentage by 20%	Work on tossing the ball to the same height at least 30 times before and after practice
Get voted "best work ethic" at end of season	Increase intensity at practice to noticeable level at least 3 out of 5 days	Practice skills 30 minutes before & after practice 3 days a week

climb, their ultimate goal is to reach the top of the mountain. However, once they commence climbing, they focus very little, if any, on the pinnacle. It still may provide direction and purpose, but it can be very detrimental if they focus on the outcome (getting to the top) instead of focusing on the process (their next immediate move). If the climber is focused on the ledge 25 feet above, he may miss the loose rock right in front of his face.

This is true for rock climbers, or any athlete focused too far in the future. Goals help you see what the future may look like, but if you forget about what you have to do in the present, you will never reach the top. A coach once told her team, "If your heads are at the Final Four, your butts will be home." In other words, if you are only focused on the outcome, you will not be engaged in the present or execute the steps needed to get you to the end.

Record Your Goals

As mentioned earlier, many people *set* goals, but few actually *achieve* them. The problem is most people stop at step one. The next step to quality goal-setting is to write the goals in an obvious location, forcing you to see them regularly. Athletes tape their goals to their bathroom mirrors or put them on bulletin boards in their rooms. Others place them in a drawer or in their backpack. It really does not matter where you put them as long as you can see them on a consistent basis. By putting goals on paper, you create accountability. There is something about seeing your goals in writing, in front of you each day that helps encourage behavior change. Instead of just saying you "hope" something happens, now you are saying, "If I do this, I'll make it happen."

Share Your Goals

In addition to creating a visual reminder, it also helps to tell others your plan. Choose someone you trust to share your goals with, and review them with this person on a regular basis. Like writing them down, sharing goals will help hold you accountable to achieving them. Knowing someone else knows your plan will encourage you to follow through. Think about it. Whoever you tell is likely to ask about your progress. This should increase your motivation and inclination to do the necessary work.

We challenge you to commit to this process for one season. You have nothing to lose. It has been proven effective for athletes disciplined enough to follow through. Rather than just thinking about what you want, set appropriate goals and develop a plan to achieve them. Your willingness and dedication to this strategy will demonstrate how serious and committed you truly are about reaching your potential.

Develop Quality Practice Habits

In addition to setting goals, athletes must work to develop quality practice habits. Too often athletes say they are committed, but during practices they appear to be "off" or just going through the motions. In reality, practice is the time to prepare to compete at the highest possible level on a consistent basis. Therefore, athletes must learn how to turn themselves "on" and develop habits that produce quality training sessions. It is tough to stay focused day in and day out of practice, but it is crucial for reaching your potential. Therefore, the following three practice habits will be discussed in this section to help you better utilize and maximize your training, while demonstrating your true commitment to the sport.

- Have a Purpose for Practice
- Incorporate Imagery into Your Training
- Compartmentalize Your Life

Coaches constantly talk about commitment and sacrifice for your sport. We want you to recognize that we agree such qualities are essential in order to be a successful athlete, but you will notice that we conclude this section discussing the importance of maintaining a healthy balance because although it is necessary to work hard and sacrifice, it is also crucial to find balance between life and sport.

Have a Purpose for Practice

*You're either getting better or getting worse each day.
There is no such thing as coasting as an athlete.*

If you are not improving, someone else may be catching up. Whether it is an opponent getting faster, stronger and more skilled, or a fellow teammate vying for your position, the reality is that if you are not improving, there is a very good chance you are losing ground. Whether you are the athlete trying to keep your top position, or you are the one trying to grab a starting spot, the key to making daily strides is having a purpose for each practice. You might think this is obvious. However, we have discovered that few athletes make it a point to identify a purpose for practice and use that purpose to guide their focus. Many athletes go to practice, go through the motions, and go home. They may not make a conscious effort to change this behavior because they are more physically talented than others and they can "get away" with not being purposeful with their practice. Some athletes might not do it because they never really thought about it or they think it is not important. Others assume coaches create the purpose through practice, while some athletes just lack the discipline to do it. Do any of these describe you? Remember, purposeful behavior leads to measurable gains and a better understanding and awareness of your strengths, weaknesses and level over time.

A purpose can relate to the task, the skill, your emotions or your intensity. There is no right or wrong purpose. Instead, it is what you need to get you through and make you better that day. Challenge yourself to never have a workout, weight room session, practice session, or mental training session without a purpose. For example, you might focus on:

- The timing of a skill you must perform in pressure situations (skill)
- Communicating more effectively with teammates during a scrimmage (task)
- Responding more appropriately to feedback from coaches (emotion)
- Increasing effort during conditioning at the end of practice (intensity)

A collegiate golfer was having difficulty focusing for three hours of practice every day, hitting ball after ball. At the end of the day if you asked him about practice, he would say it was fine, but it you asked him what he specifically worked on or improved, his response was vague. In an effort to change, he began selecting a purpose each day. One day his purpose was to take each shot as if it was in competition (never taking more than one of the same type of shot in a row). Another day his purpose was to improve self-talk. Even on structured days he selected his own measurable purpose based around coach's practice plan. Each day he took a moment before practice to identify a purpose and write a reminder on his hand. Over time, he went from going through the motions to actually enjoying and improving his game.

When identifying a purpose for practice, you should not ignore all other aspects of your performance. That would be counter-productive. The purpose merely gives you one area to pay closer attention to that day. Some athletes focus on skill execution, others focus on speed and intensity, while some make their purpose finding the fun each day. Regardless of the topic, the purpose helps keep you focused and it helps create variety in your approach to practice, ultimately discouraging you from just going through the motions.

Having a purpose also can help you be smart about your training by allowing you to regulate intensity and rest when necessary. Specifically, your purpose may be to allow your body to recover so you perform fewer repetitions that day. This is not an easy concept for all athletes as they tend to think "more is always better." In other words, if I work longer and harder than anyone else, I will always have an edge over them. While this mindset can be admirable and at times lead to greater performances, it also can lead to injury, burn-out or a slump in performance.

A track athlete had this mindset. Her purpose was to work harder and longer than her competition to gain the edge. She began doing extra workouts outside of the training regimen designed by her coach. Her performance began to suffer as she struggled with overuse injuries. It was difficult for her to understand how her mindset was contributing to her inability to perform on race days. However, once she relinquished the idea that more is always better, her performances began to consistently improve and she became healthier.

Take enough pride in what you are doing as an athlete to train with a purpose every day. Do not cheat yourself, your teammates or your coaches because you are just going through the motions. But keep in mind there is a fine line between working hard and over training. Communicate with your coaches, trainers and others to see if it is okay to do extra work. If it is okay, put in the extra time because it could help you gain an edge. If not, your purpose must shift to rest, recovery, or your mental game so your physical training will be more effective the next time.

You might also think about sharing your purpose with a teammate or coach each day to again build in some accountability. Much like telling someone your goals, sharing your purpose will increase the likelihood that you will engage in purposeful training. As well, you could keep a daily log or calendar and make a check or an X on the day representing "purposeful practice" or "no purpose in practice." By checking yourself in this way, you more honestly can assess what you are "really" doing as opposed to what you "think" you are doing. This behavior will demonstrate a more consistent commitment to yourself or your team.

Incorporate Imagery into your Training

In addition to the previously mentioned strategies, incorporating imagery into your training also can improve your performance. Imagery is the creation or re-creation of an event or picture in your mind. Athletes often imagine themselves performing a particular way before it happens, or replay effective performances in their minds.

Michael Jordan was the best basketball player on the planet

during his prime. Jordan speaks in great detail about how he would see himself playing against opponents long before they stepped on the court. He would picture himself dominating opponents, minimizing their strengths and exploiting their weaknesses. This preparation put him in a positive state of mind prior to the game and allowed his instincts to take over during the game because he felt like he had already been there. There are countless examples of successful athletes who attribute part of their success to being able to see themselves competing at a high level before it actually happens. Following are two strategies that might enhance this aspect of your preparation.

Image Rather Than Visualize

When most athletes talk about visualizing a performance, they are referring to "seeing" themselves perform. It is more effective if you can incorporate as many of the other senses as possible. For example, swimmers should recall the smell of the chlorine or feel the texture of the tile on their feet. Golfers should smell the fresh cut grass and feel the wind, heat or rain. Baseball players should hear the crack of the bat as they solidly contact the ball. Gymnasts should hear the music and feel the rotations of their bodies twisting through the air. The key to effective imagery is using as many of the senses as possible. The more vivid the image, the more likely it will be "imprinted" into your brain. This creates the illusion of "been there, done that!" As well, imagery can help you improve confidence, prepare for various situations and environments, and help invoke a more positive emotional state or arousal level during or prior to competition or practice.

Just like any physical skill, imagery must be practiced to be improved. Use the five minutes before you go to sleep at night to practice your imagery. Use all your senses and imagine yourself performing skills in your sport exceptionally well.

Notice your surroundings, your mood and energy level as you see and feel yourself performing. To improve your images, videotape yourself, watch the performance, then close your eyes and feel and see yourself doing it again. The more you practice, the more proficient you will become and when the real situation arises, you will feel like a veteran.

Incorporate Imagery into Every Practice Session

What do you think about during down time in practice? What happens in those moments just after you perform a skill very well? Those are great moments to practice your imagery. For instance, we encourage baseball players to pause for a moment after making solid contact with the ball in batting practice. During this brief (2–3 seconds) pause, we want them to replay the moment from reading the pitch to hitting the ball. You can do the same in field hockey by pausing to recall a great shot on goal as you return to the line in a shooting drill. In golf, take a moment to recall the feel and sound of a smooth and effective swing. In whatever sport you compete, pause for a few seconds after performing a skill well and recreate the image in your mind. This process will program your brain so you will be more likely to replicate the skill or movement in a competitive environment. Instead of one great shot, imagery allows you to experience two in one!

Remember how we said more is not always better. Imagery also provides a way to get extra practice without the physical demand. For example, gymnastics is a grueling sport on the body. It requires the use of almost every muscle and there is a great chance for injury if athletes are tired. Therefore, gymnasts can imagine themselves performing a perfect beam, bars or floor routine before and after the actual physical practice. This technique provides additional practice and a chance to build confidence as they see and feel themselves performing the skills successfully. This is important for other physically demanding sports as well as situations when you cannot actually perform. Imagery can be used when out with an injury or when venues and situations do not allow for actual physical practice. For example, imagery can be used when the fields are frozen, you are experiencing a rain delay, or your bus is running late and you do not have the regular hour time allotted for warm-up. Imagery can help prepare you in those situations allowing you to feel ready when it comes time to compete. Taken together, imagery added to athletes' regular practice can provide greater gains and a better likelihood of reaching their potential than physical practice alone.

Compartmentalize Your Life

Be here when you are here and
be there when you are there.

Whether it is learning to focus on being a student while in class or an athlete on the field, another critical skill to develop is known as compartmentalizing. Compartmentalizing concerns one's ability to separate aspects of life at will. This process encourages full focus in a single setting by letting go of irrelevant or useless thoughts from a separate situation or setting.

It is amazing the number and variety of non-sport specific thoughts that invade the minds of athletes during practice. They are distracted by thoughts of food, significant others, family, the weather and more. According to many of the student-athletes we consult, school is one of the most pervasive and distracting thoughts. Doing well in school is important to many student-athletes and they often bring those concerns to practice. Interestingly, when asked what they think about during class or while studying, these same athletes cite their sport.

Do you see anything wrong with this picture? While at

practice, do you have any control over the history exam you did poorly on or how much work you have to do tomorrow? Similarly, while studying for the exam, do you have control over what happened in practice or at the competition earlier in the day? The answer to both of these questions is "no." And let's face it, as much as you might like to think you have control over your girlfriend or boyfriend during practice, you truly have no control. Thus, whether your thoughts stray to a fight you had, what you want for dinner, or how many pages you have to read for class, the fact is not one of these thoughts will help your performance. In order to maximize your performance potential, you must learn how to compartmentalize your life. Be an athlete on the field, a student in the classroom, and a friend or family member at other times. Following are suggestions for how to transition into being an athlete.

- The Superman
- The "To Do" List
- Signing In
- Mind-Body Check

The Superman

To maximize your training sessions, you must find a method that will allow you to focus fully on what you are doing at the time. You must commit to being an athlete. One of the most effective strategies involves identifying a specific point where you physically make the transition from being a student, son or daughter, boyfriend or girlfriend to being an athlete. For example, one athlete would make it a point to walk to practice by himself and think about all of the issues and tasks that were relevant in his life at the time. He would devise a plan for how he would address each of them later that evening or the next day. Once he was ready to move beyond those issues, he would put on his practice uniform. However, in his mind this was no ordinary uniform. This was his "Superman" outfit.

Just like Clark Kent morphed into a super human upon exiting the phone booth, this athlete turned into a focused competitor when he put on his practice clothes. This may sound silly, but the strategy worked as he is now a professional basketball player in the National Basketball Association. You too can adopt a variation of this strategy by fostering a conscious thought or behavior when you put on your last piece of equipment or uniform, when you walk through the gate or enter the practice arena, or when your coach first brings the team together at the beginning of practice.

The "To-Do" List

The Duke Women's Lacrosse team has a time at the beginning of each practice designed to help them transition into "athlete." During this time each athlete is supposed to think about any issues that might bother or distract her during practice. She then must devise a quick mental plan for how she will address it later. This process relinquishes her thoughts from it now. One defender on the team makes a list in her mind of anything in her life she must address once practice is finished. She makes a schedule and then erases them one by one until they are all gone from her mind. This helps her know that she has a plan to address all of these issues later, which gives her the peace of mind to focus on practice now.

This method does not need to be completed as a team. Individual athletes have used similar techniques of writing a list of "things to do after practice." They specifically note times when those tasks will be completed or issues will be contemplated. The point must be clear to the athlete that the time represents when he or she is allowed to focus on those issues and that time is not during practice. Others write down thoughts about family, boy/girlfriends or tests that are invading their minds and put them in a "to be done later" box. This gives them permission to stop thinking about those issues now, knowing they can pull that piece of paper out after practice and deal with them.

Signing In

Another strategy that has proven effective in helping athletes move past irrelevant thoughts and enter practice or competition ready to play is "signing-in." Some coaches post a team roster on the locker room door. All members of the team sign their names upon entering the locker room to signify they are there for practice and ready to be athletes. You could create a sign-in sheet of your own and put it in your locker if your coach does not provide one for the entire team. Once you sign your name, it is a signal that you are an athlete for the next few hours and you are committed to being fully focused on making the most of that time.

Mind-Body Check

The final step toward transitioning into athlete is completing a full mind/body check. Once you have relinquished non-sport thoughts, you can check, "mind ready." Then you must notice the energy and tension in your body. Each athlete has a physical readiness that encourages optimal performance. You must identify what that means to you. Are your muscles too tight or too loose? Is your energy reserve too high or too low? Determine where you are and engage in necessary behaviors to get your body and energy where they need to be. Athletes often use music, relaxation techniques (see Embrace Pressure chapter), or imagery to help them achieve physical and mental readiness for practice. Athletes who are too tense or too hyped up will listen to calming music, take deep breaths and find a quiet place to relax for a minute or two. Athletes who are too relaxed often use "pump up" music, visualize exciting games and run around a bit to get their mind and body ready to perform. Once you have completed your mind/body check you should be ready to perform.

The strategies mentioned help athletes put aside thoughts that will not benefit them during practice (and can be used on competition days as well) and ensure their bodies are ready to go. We know that there are busy days or stressful days when work piles up, people get in fights and parents nag, but there is nothing you can do to solve those issues during practice and if you choose to focus your thoughts there, you surely cannot be focused on your sport. In addition, those thoughts can influence muscle tension and physical fatigue. Therefore, before you can have a purposeful practice, you must decide if you are actually ready and committed, body and mind, to be an athlete. We hope you can use some of these strategies to help you develop your own pre-practice (or pre-competition) routine for becoming an athlete. You might be pleasantly surprised at the difference it makes for you.

Maintain a Healthy Balance

Up to this point we have emphasized the importance of giving more than just "lip service" to commitment. We have discussed the importance of taking control of your thoughts and your behaviors to improve your performance. Without question, you will not maximize your potential if you are not willing to put in that extra effort and make some sacrifices. Typically those sacrifices are time, energy and effort. However, what many athletes do not recognize is that sacrifices also include diet, sleep, and social life. What are you willing to sacrifice while still maintaining a healthy balance? Are you willing to eat properly? Are you willing to stop drinking alcohol? Will you be the first to leave the party to ensure you get enough rest? What are you willing to say "no" to in order to make a commitment to excel in your sport? If it is detrimental to your performance and you still do it, are you truly committed? Of course it is important to remember that being committed does not require you give up everything. A committed athlete can still have fun and a social life outside of sport. The solution is to find a healthy and productive balance.

Many athletes lose perspective on what it means to be committed. We know numerous athletes who take their eating habits to an extreme. They may run extra or engage in disordered eating, claiming a desire to excel in their sport. The truth is these individuals are not committed because these are dangerous and unhealthy behaviors more likely to trigger injury or illness than enhanced performance. Ask yourself, is your eating and exercise behavior intended to improve your chances on a high fashion runway or in your competitive arena? Are you working to improve how you look in a swimsuit or how you perform in your uniform? Similarly, ask yourself, "Am I obsessed with my sport or committed to my sport?" Some athletes are so focused on being athletes that they end up with no social life and few, if any, friends outside their teams. None of these are healthy behaviors. Once again, the key to a healthy commitment is to strive for a healthy balance.

Have Other Passions

One way to achieve this healthy balance is to have other passions in your life other than your sport. If you do not have other passions, life can be great as long as your sport is going well, you are playing the role you want on the team and you are healthy. However, life may not be as enjoyable when your sport is not going well, you are not playing your preferred role and you are sick or injured. It can be very unhealthy when your sport is the only place from which you draw satisfaction, confidence and your identity. Athletes need to find alternatives. For example, learning to play a musical instrument, volunteering time for a worthy cause or making it a point to develop friendships with people outside athletics will help create balance.

Find something that will give you a sense of purpose outside your role as an athlete. This will help you maintain perspective when your sport is not going as well as you might like.

Terrell Davis played professional football for the Denver Broncos and had a great career. Unfortunately, his career was cut short because of bad knees. When asked if he was going to miss being a football player, he said he would miss being with his teammates and the camaraderie that goes along with being a member of a team; however, he was not just a football player. Davis went on to say that playing football was something he did with much passion and intensity, but he had other passions in his life and he wanted to pursue those further now that football was finished. In essence, he was saying that while football was very important to him and he worked hard to be successful, it did not completely define who he was as a person.

Contrary to Davis's perspective, several former collegiate athletes claimed personal regrets over not having enough balance in their lives during their time as student-athletes. They explained being wholly absorbed in college athletics and missing out on other experiences and opportunities afforded to college students. They regretted only having athlete friends or going to athlete parties. They regretted not going abroad or attending special events at the school.

Having balance is easier said than done as these athletes did not even realize their mistakes until long after their athletic careers had ended. It is important to grasp the idea that your time is precious and time away from your sport should be used wisely. You should find what is important to you outside of sport and make sure you are spending some time there. A quick check can be done by answering the following question: "What is most important to me in my life other than my sport?" If you thought of something, but you do not spend time on it, then you need to transfer some time to that aspect of your life. You will not have much extra time, but even a small amount of time doing something else you enjoy is better than none. This will help you live a quality life that is well balanced when your athletic career is not going well or it is finished.

In conclusion, to be truly committed you cannot just say you are committed. You must engage in behaviors that demonstrate your dedication to the sport. Sometimes you have to do the extra work others do not want to do. Other times you have to use quality practice strategies or train more efficiently and effectively. All the while, you have to be able to maintain a proper perspective while engaging in healthy behaviors. You certainly will come closer to reaching your potential if you can do all that.

To help you have a better idea of your current level of commitment, we have provided two commitment surveys at the end of this chapter. One is designed for you to complete. The other is designed for your coach to complete based on his or her perceptions of your current commitment level. Take a few minutes to complete the one designed for you and then ask your coach to evaluate you. It is important that both of you are completely honest. The resulting scores will provide insight into whether or not you are truly committed. In addition, you should take the time to discuss the results with your coach and devise a plan accordingly.

Key Points to Remember

1. Determination and pride are the foundation for commitment.

2. Set performance and process goals in addition to outcome goals.

3. Use imagery to enhance your practice, confidence and performance.

4. Be disciplined enough to have a purpose each time you train.

5. Compartmentalize your life to allow for complete focus in the moment, whether that is in or out of sport.

6. Maintain a healthy balance between commitment to your sport and life.

7. Remember, having balance does not mean you are less committed. It just means you are being wise and you are likely to have a longer, more productive career.

8. Take a moment to review your answers to the questions at the beginning of the chapter. What changes can you make to improve your commitment level?

Commitment Survey Self-Assessment

On a scale from one to five, rate yourself on your level of commitment to becoming a great athlete.

1	2	3	4	5
Strongly Disagree	Disagree	Undecided	Agree	Strongly Agree

___ I consistently demonstrate an unwavering determination to succeed.

___ I regularly ask coaches to come to practice early, stay late, or work on individual skills with me.

___ I consistently engage in behaviors that help me improve as an athlete.

___ I never "cut corners" in my training.

___ I consistently set outcome as well as process and performance goals.

___ I record my goals and regularly evaluate my progress.

___ I consistently come to practice in a good mood and look forward to training.

___ I consistently have a purpose for my training that helps me stay focused.

___ I am consistently willing to sacrifice aspects of my life that are detrimental to my performance.

___ I consistently have a balanced perspective on my sport and life outside sport.

___ **Total**

Score

45–50 Excellent Commitment: You demonstrate a high level of commitment and have a balanced perspective. Keep up the good work.

40–44 Very Good Commitment: You are committed. Make sure you address any areas that you need to improve.

30–39 Concern Regarding Commitment: There are several areas of commitment that are lacking. It is important to address these areas immediately or you are unlikely to succeed in your sport.

1–29 Total Lack of Commitment: You are not committed. You must make significant changes immediately or you will certainly not succeed in your sport.

Commitment Survey: Coach Version

Name of Athlete: _____

On a scale from one to five, rate this athlete on his/her level of commitment to becoming a great athlete.

1	2	3	4	5
Strongly Disagree	Disagree	Undecided	Agree	Strongly Agree

___ Consistently demonstrates an unwavering determination to succeed.

___ Regularly asks coaches to come early, stay late, or practice individual skills.

___ Consistently engages in behaviors that help him/her improve as an athlete.

___ Never "cuts corners" in training.

___ Consistently sets outcome as well as process and performance goals.

___ Records goals and regularly evaluates his/her progress.

___ Consistently comes to practice in a good mood and looks forward to training.

___ Consistently has a purpose for training that helps him/her stay focused.

___ Is consistently willing to change behaviors that are detrimental to performance.

___ Consistently has a balanced perspective on his/her sport and life outside sport.

___ **Total**

Score

45–50 Excellent Commitment: Your coach feels you are committed at the highest level and you have a balanced perspective. Keep up the good work.

40–44 Very Good Commitment: Your coach feels you are committed. Make a commitment to improve any areas that you need to improve.

30–39 Concern Regarding Commitment: Your coach has real concerns about your commitment. You need to communicate with him/her and begin to change your commitment or you are unlikely to succeed in your sport.

1–29 Total Lack of Commitment: Your coach views you as demonstrating a complete lack of commitment. You should take drastic measures to improve your commitment or you will certainly not succeed in your sport.

Believe in Yourself

Nobody can make you feel inferior without your consent.

ELEANOR ROOSEVELT

If you hear a voice within you say "you cannot paint," then by all means paint, and that voice will be silenced.

VINCENT VAN GOGH

Think About It

Take a moment to begin examining your confidence by answering the following questions:

Does your sense of confidence come from within?

Do you view confidence as a gift and look to others to give it to you?

Do you spend more time developing your weaknesses or strengths?

Can you "act" confidently when you do not feel confident?

Do you feel more confident when you know you are prepared?

Do you struggle being positive with yourself when your performance is not going well?

onfidence is a fragile, yet incredibly important aspect of consistent, high level performance. Great athletes have a very strong belief in themselves and their ability to perform well in most situations. This belief is deep-rooted and not easily undermined. Athletes who lack this deep-rooted belief tend to depend very heavily on other people for how they feel about themselves. They look to their coaches, teammates, parents and others to reassure them or enhance their confidence. The problem with relying on others to boost your confidence is you cannot control when, where, how or if they will do it when you need it. It is true that others can create an environment that enhances your confidence. However, your level of confidence in any situation ultimately is up to you. The following techniques are offered to help you build confidence.

- Spend More Time Developing Strengths than Weaknesses
- Focus on the Process
- Know You are Prepared
- Fake It Till You Make It
- Coach Yourself Up

Spend More Time Developing Strengths than Weaknesses

According to Marcus Buckingham, a world-renowned researcher, author and speaker, individuals have a much better chance to grow and improve in areas of strength compared to areas of weakness. Therefore, he argues we should spend more time developing strengths than weaknesses. It is important to clarify that he is not saying to ignore weaknesses or major flaws in your repertoire of skills considering such an approach could keep you from making the line-up. He is saying that sometimes we sacrifice the development of our strengths by focusing too heavily on developing our weaknesses. For example, a high school basketball player who has a great jump shot from twelve to fifteen feet, but is not a great ball handler, should certainly work on his ball handling skills. However, he should not spend so much time trying to develop that part of his game that he sacrifices his development as an outside shooter. Another example would be a sprinter in track and field who naturally has a great start out of the blocks but spends most of her time in practice on the last ten meters of a hurdle race because that is her "weakest" phase of the race. She very likely can improve the end of the race, but more of her time might have been better spent fine tuning her start.

Please do not tell your coach we said you do not have to work on your weaknesses. That is not what we are saying. The main point is more time should be focused on developing your strengths because that is where you have the most potential for growth. As you hone your strengths, you will experience more successes, which breeds greater confidence. The more confident you are, the better you will likely perform overall.

Focus on the Process

It is easy to stay confident when your performances are going well and you are winning. It is more difficult to stay confident through losses, errors and poor performances. However, if you can shift your focus from the end result to the process, you will give yourself more chances to boost confidence throughout your athletic career. If a wrestler only evaluates his ability based on number of pins, he misses out on noticing improvements in technique and strategy over the season. If a lacrosse player gauges her success on total number of minutes played, she might not notice the improvements she has made in her skills and how she helped her teammates get better throughout the year. Similarly, if athletes only measure success by final win-loss record, they may miss several confidence building opportunities encountered throughout the season.

There are relatively few competitions in comparison to practices and only one person or team wins at the end of the day. There also are limited spots or positions to fill for each competition. This is why we spoke earlier about using process goals. By focusing on the process as opposed to the outcome, you direct your attention to what you do well, rather than who you beat or who beat you. You begin to evaluate your performance based on successful completion of a task or improvement over time. For example, a softball player may have a low batting average, which could negatively influence her confidence. If she stays focused on the final number, she does not give herself many opportunities to see improvements or build her confidence. However, if she focuses on technique changes or swinging at good pitches, she has more chances to succeed and improve. Similarly, a swimmer may not be winning many races and his focus on losses may diminish his confidence. If he were to shift his focus to aspects of his race he can improve (e.g., smoother turns, longer strokes), he would give himself more opportunities to be successful and build confidence. Again, a more confident athlete likely will lead to a more effective athlete.

Shannon Rowbury, a former NCAA indoor mile champion, 2008 Olympian, and 2009 World Championship bronze medalist in the 1500 meters, is a great example of an athlete who shifted her focus from outcomes (winning, beating other runners) to the process of running well. Shannon began focusing on the process by developing a race plan that she could commit to following each time she raced. She would break the mile or 1500 meter race into three distinct phases and establish brief focus cues for each phase. Her cue for phase 1 was "good rhythm." During phase 2 she would say "stay strong and breathe." And, with 200 meters to go, Shannon would say "my time." After much practice, she was able to refine the plan and her cues, giving her the feeling it belonged to her. This new focus allowed her to enter competitions with much more confidence. Shannon now was focused on her plan, not winning or other runners. In addition, she could increase confidence even if she did not win because she could identify areas of improvement or good performances. In other words, even on days when the entire race did not go as planned, she still was able to identify one phase or one part that did go well.

Regardless of your sport, allow yourself a chance to be successful by focusing on the process of performing not just the outcomes. Recognizing the small steps and little victories each day (e.g., taking the ball on the move in lacrosse or being more aggressive as a wrestler) can help increase confidence over time. This in turn, will allow you to consistently perform at a higher level because you will be focused on practicing and honing your skills rather than winning or losing.

Know You Are Prepared

Quality preparation plays a critical role in building confidence. You will feel more prepared and confident if you know in your heart you devoted the necessary time to develop your mind and body. This is very similar to taking exams in school. If you study long and hard rather than cramming at the last minute, you will be more confident in your ability to do well on the exam. Work hard, work smart, and you will be more confident when the time comes to test your skills.

This concept sounds very simple. However, we are amazed at the number of athletes who are quick to blame a lack of success or even their struggles with confidence on someone else or something outside their control. If you are struggling with confidence, maybe you are not truly putting in quality training time. Can you honestly say you are as prepared as you can possibly be given your current situation? If not, this is the time to make changes. Take responsibility and do not make excuses for yourself when it comes to this very important aspect of building confidence.

A college athlete returned from summer vacation and was very nervous about passing the pre-season running test. Ultimately she failed the test and was forced to engage in extra morning workouts until she passed. This athlete was upset and frustrated. She said she just was not confident in her running ability. In truth, this athlete did not put in enough time or effort on her summer workouts, leaving her unprepared for the test. Had she taken more time to prepare, she would have been more confident because she would have known she had the strength and speed required to pass. Do not cheat yourself by slacking on workouts and then blame confidence. It is a fact and a promise that you will not be confident in your ability to perform well in your sport if you have not put in the necessary work.

Fake It Till You Make It

There may be times when you have tried everything else, yet still you do not feel confident. For those moments, it is important you learn how to act confident. Many young athletes join teams with upperclassmen already at the helm. The younger athletes may not be confident yet as their positions are unknown and they have not proven themselves. Situations like that might require a little faking. Tell yourself you have the skill and you can play with the best of them (even though inside you are questioning those very statements). Walk onto the field and ask for the ball. Take the lead even when you really want to hide. In other words, fake the mindset and engage in the behaviors that make you appear confident. Actually *do* the opposite of what you feel.

A NCAA Division I Men's Soccer player had to act confident when his role was switched from three year starter to athlete with limited playing time. The situation negatively influenced his confidence when he began thinking too much about his performance and doubting his ability. He felt like he had to play perfectly in order to stay in the game. This athlete wanted to regain his confidence so he could "just play" like he did in the past. He shifted his focus from "I never get the chance to play" or "I'm not good enough to play" to "I will be ready to play when I get the chance." He made a deliberate effort to act more confidently while warming up by running with his head up, shoulders back and moving with authority. He also walked with an air of confidence as he approached the official to be substituted in the game. Once on the field he acted assertively from the start, making strong runs to gain possession of free balls and attacking 50/50 balls. It was amazing the difference it made in his body language and ultimately his play. He began to play more freely and subsequently gained more playing time and real confidence. He even earned his starting spot again.

Similarly, a third line mid-fielder in lacrosse would enter the game hoping not to make any mistakes for fear of being yelled at or pulled from the game. He played tentatively and guided the ball when passing. It had a huge impact on his performance. He became frustrated with his lack of confidence and decided he wanted to change his approach. Again, this athlete made a conscious effort to "act" like he wanted to have the ball thrown to him by moving more forcefully to get open and being available to receive balls from his teammates. He also began "acting" like he wanted to be on the field late in the game. He would tell himself he was ready and he hoped coach would put him in. This change of behavior eventually led to a change of attitude, which ultimately impacted his confidence and play. By faking confidence early on, he eventually started to feel confident.

Shannon Rowbury, the 1500 meter runner, used this tactic to help her feel more confident and relaxed at the beginning of races. As part of her race plan she would smile at the start line and tell herself, "There is no other place in the world I would rather be than right here, right now." Even though she might not feel totally confident in those situations, by smiling and "acting" like she wanted to be there, it helped her take the edge off.

Finally, a female collegiate tennis player lacked confidence on the court. Each time she stepped out to play, she would look across the court and immediately identify all her opponent's strengths, which basically psyched her out before play even began. Her shoulders would slump. She would not make eye contact and she would look scared. She attempted to change her mindset by creating an on-court alter-ego who demonstrated the qualities she wanted to possess. This athlete wanted to be strong, confident and powerful. She selected the image of "Zena–Warrior Princess" as her guide. She viewed this character as confident and unafraid, so she faked those qualities when she stepped on the court. When acting like the character, she hit harder and went after shots. She would not second guess or hold back. These behaviors ultimately changed her play and eventually her own mentality. After time she actually adopted the qualities she had been faking.

The reality is that you are not going to feel confident at all times. The next time you are struggling with your confidence in any part of your life, try faking it. Carry yourself with a little more authority. Hold your head up and your shoulders back and act like you are going to be successful. By not allowing yourself to hesitate or second guess yourself, you just might see you actually have the skills and ability to succeed. After a while you will not need to fake it anymore.

Coach Yourself Up

We all talk to ourselves and on many occasions these comments are negative, cruel and self-defeating. We make statements like, "I suck," "I can't do this," "I never beat her," "They are much bigger than us," and "I have never competed well here before." Although you may not feel these words are too influential, the truth is these messages set you up to fail. They focus your attention on what you cannot do, while confirming feelings of inadequacy. The more you tell yourself you are incapable, the more you will believe your own words. This in turn negatively impacts your behavior, effort and persistence toward improving a skill. Why should I put out more effort in practice when I know "I can't do it" anyway?

Use your imagination for this next exercise. Think about a situation when you performed poorly, made a mistake or felt you let down the team. Once you have the situation in mind, reflect on all of the negative comments you made to yourself. Now, think about a respected teammate making the exact same mistake and "letting the team down." Next, imagine yourself talking to him or her the same way you talked to yourself moments ago. You also can imagine this teammate talking to you the same way you talked to yourself after the mistake. The likelihood is you made comments such as "You are a &%$# idiot," "That was the worst shot I have ever seen," "You are pitiful," or "You will never beat her."

Think about it. Would you truly talk to your teammate that way? What would you do if one your teammates actually talked to you the way you talk to yourself after a mistake? Most athletes admit they would not allow a teammate to talk that way nor would they talk to one of their teammates in that manner. The question then becomes, "Why would you talk to yourself that way?" Many athletes are much harder on themselves than they are on others because they know they can get away with it and they think it will help push them to avoid making the same mistake again. The reality is this type of self-talk is ultimately detrimental to consistent high level performance because it is detrimental to confidence.

What about you? Do you struggle with negative self-talk? We challenge you to work on this skill if you are ever to reach your potential. If you continually tell yourself you suck, you are pitiful or you cannot do something, you will eventually believe it and your performance will mirror that belief. Therefore, you must practice being more positive with your internal dialogue to build confidence over time.

An effective strategy is to write down positive comments, statements or thoughts and post them on your wall. These comments may have come from others. Perhaps your coach complimented your dribbling skills or your friend said you defended well the other day. But the bulk of these comments should be your own. Post comments you thought about yourself, but were too embarrassed to share with others. Maybe you came back from far behind in a cross country race or you made a great shot out of really high rough in golf. Remind yourself of your successes, not just your failures. Build yourself up. Do not wait for others to do it for you.

Filling Your Confidence Tank

An effective tool to use when thinking about confidence is what we call "the confidence tank." We have athletes imagine they are carrying a confidence tank or reservoir around with them on a daily basis. There are two openings in this tank. There is the opening at the top where you fill the tank and an opening on the bottom where you drain the tank. When preparing yourself to practice or compete, it is important for your confidence tank to be full. Unfortunately, we often see athletes who continuously drain their tanks with negative self-talk and self-doubt, while doing very little to refill the tank. As an athlete it is important to implement the strategies we have suggested in this section so that you can fill your confidence tank to an optimal level. This is not about being cocky or obnoxious. This is about admitting your strengths and using them to propel yourself forward.

One last factor to consider regarding your confidence tank

concerns compliments. While we have encouraged you to avoid depending on others for your confidence, you also should not discount compliments or recognitions of your performance by those you respect. Think about it. If you are not being positive with yourself and you discount compliments others provide you, your tank will always be running low or on empty. Therefore, listen to positive feedback from others and take their words to heart. Plug the opening at the bottom, stop draining your tank and give yourself a chance to feel good about yourself and your performance.

Confidence is a critical component of consistent, high level performance and overall athlete satisfaction. Great athletes tend to have a strong belief in their abilities to succeed and therefore often perform at a high level because they keep trying and keep fighting through numerous failures and mistakes. They do not dwell on mistakes because they know they can improve or correct them with a bit more work or effort. These athletes do not depend too heavily on others for their confidence; instead they believe in themselves because they know they put in the necessary work. As well, confident athletes provide themselves more confidence building opportunities by focusing on the process more than the outcome. And although they were not all born naturally confident, they were able to build up a belief in themselves by practicing the skills mentioned here. We encourage you to learn from them so you might be more confident as you train and compete.

Key Points to Remember

1. Spending more time developing strengths than weaknesses builds confidence and enhances performance.

2. Focusing on the process of performance rather than the outcome allows you to feel more in control and confident.

3. Confidence is not a gift, so avoid depending too heavily on others to give it to you.

4. Sometimes you have to act your way into feeling confident (smile and stand tall even if you do not feel it right away).

5. Coach yourself "up." When you are struggling, talk to yourself like you would talk to a struggling teammate.

6. Take a moment to review your answers to the questions at the beginning of the chapter. What changes can you make to improve your confidence?

Embrace the Pressure

I've missed more than 9000 shots in my career. I've lost almost 300 games. 26 times, I've been trusted to take the game winning shot and missed. I've failed over and over and over again in my life. And that is why I succeed.
MICHAEL JORDAN

The person who gets the farthest is generally the one who is willing to do and dare. The sure-thing boat never gets far from shore.
DALE CARNEGIE

Think About it

Take a moment to begin examining how you handle pressure by answering the following questions:

Do you get nervous before "big" competitions?

Do you look forward to situations that you perceive to be filled with pressure?

Are you "cool and calm" under pressure or do you let them see you sweat?

What happens to your body and mind when you feel the pressure rise?

Do you care "too much" about the outcome of a competition?

Are you overly focused on how you might be perceived by others?

A top college golfer approaches an 8 ft. putt on the third hole of a playoff. She has worked very hard since she was 13 years old to be in this moment and this putt could win the national championship for her team and give her the individual title as well. The rain begins to fall and there is a tense silence among the crowd. Everyone is watching as she reads the putt. Her head is filled with numerous thoughts before she is finally ready. She approaches, putts the ball and sinks it in the heart of the cup. She wins the tournament.

It's the most important game of the season as the outcome dictates who will compete for the national championship. His team is down by one when the kicking team approaches the field. There is only one second left on the clock and it is up to the kicker to win or lose the game. They are about to begin when the opponent's coach calls a time-out. He knows they are trying to freeze him and he knows his team's chance to play in the championship game is up to him. After the time-out he walks back to the field and drills it dead center of the uprights.

How would you respond in those situations? Would you think about all you could lose or whether you would miss, or would you see it as the best challenge you could possibly have? Would you be afraid of failing or would you embrace the pressure? The following chapter will focus on:

- Physical & psychological responses to pressure
- How you define pressure
- Becoming an athlete who embraces pressure
- Letting go of mistakes
- Learning to relax

Physical & Psychological Responses to Pressure

Athletes respond both physically and mentally to perceived pressure situations. Physical responses involve changes in the body, including changes in heart rate, blood pressure, sweating, and muscular tension. If a person interprets the situation positively, he will maintain a normal heart rate and blood pressure and have appropriate muscle tension. However, if a person feels the pressure as a negative then heart rate and blood pressure rise too much leaving the athlete more tired than she should be. These athletes also tend to sweat more and have tight muscles. It is clearly not ideal to perform a bar routine in gymnastics or throw a touchdown pass in football when your muscles are already too tight.

In addition to physical responses, athletes also incur psychological responses to perceived pressure. If an athlete interprets the situation in a negative way, detrimental thoughts and fear may follow. These are the times when you think "I can't do this," "what if I miss," or "he's watching me." These thoughts are distracting to athletes who are now focused on what they might do wrong instead of what they can do well. These thoughts take athletes' minds off what they can control, focusing them instead on extraneous variables like other people or outcomes. Of course, there are many athletes who interpret these situations positively and their thoughts stay on the game, the moment and what they can do. In fact, larger crowds, screaming fans, and event banners help put some athletes in game mode. What about you? Do you embrace these moments and feel the excitement of a good competition or do you crumble when the pressure rises?

How Do You Define Pressure?

Pressure situations are typically those deemed "more important" or holding more weight than others. Life is full of these moments. Some people feel the greatest pressure exists during athletic competitions. Others feel pressure when they have to talk in front of a large crowd. Pressure situations exist for lawyers attempting to keep their clients out of prison and doctors trying to keep their patients alive on the operating table. Anytime the expectations are high, pressure may exist. Athletes typically claim pressure rises in certain games (i.e., "the big game"), in larger venues, or when significant others (e.g., parents, scouts, friends) are watching. Many athletes believe that others put pressure on them. They feel pressure from parents who constantly sing their praises. They feel pressure from coaches touting the importance of winning a particular game. And, they feel pressure to perform when a good performance could mean getting a scholarship to college or a significant signing bonus. The fact is these situations may count more or have greater consequences, but only you can define them as "pressure." Therefore, it is important to understand and embrace the idea that pressure ultimately comes from only one place . . . YOU. You have the choice to allow those factors to stress you and you have the power to embrace and enjoy the challenge.

It's All in Your Interpretation

What is the difference between taking a penalty shot at the beginning of a game or in the last five seconds of a game when your team is losing by a point? What is the difference between taking the first serve in volleyball or serving for match point? What is the difference between competing in front of 100 people compared to 50,000 people or competing in front of friends versus strangers? Some college lacrosse teams compete in front of crowds ranging from 500–3500 people during the regular season, but 60,000 people at the Final Four. These athletes note the difference in crowd, venue, point in the game, or time of season as factors that influence pressure.

When the USA Track and Field team traveled to Italy to compete in the Junior World Championships, some of the athletes thought the competition was going to be tougher than anything they had experienced because of the size of the stadium and the perceived level of competitors they would face. In reality, these were the best going to compete against the best, but nothing else had changed. They were not expected to do anything different. The track was not longer and the hurdles were not higher. In fact, the only difference in all the situations mentioned is the athlete's interpretation. If athletes view the situation as overwhelming, they will be overwhelmed and performances will suffer. If, on the other hand, they view the situation as exciting, they will be able to stay focused on the task and perform to their potential.

Have To vs. Want To

Whether it is the first game of the season against a minor opponent or the final game of the season against your biggest rival, the skills you must perform remain the same. The basket is just as high, the goal is just as big, and the pool is just as long. The only change in these situations happens in your mind. Rather than focusing on following through, seeing the ball, or maintaining your stride, you now think, "I HAVE TO make the shot," "we HAVE TO score a goal," and "I HAVE TO stop the ball." Rather than focusing on your technique and the game, you notice the scout in the stands, your parents in the bleachers or what your coach may be thinking. You make the situation pressure filled, when in truth it is just another competition. This "big game" mentality ultimately shifts your focus from the task to the environment, and from enjoying the competition to hoping you do not fail. Once you recognize there truly is no difference outside of your own head, it is easier to refocus on what you can do and what you will do, not what you HAVE TO do. Gary Mack explained this idea when he said,

"The likelihood of something occurring is more likely to occur if you can let go of the need for it to occur" (Mack, 2001).

It is possible to want something too much. In those situations people tend to try too hard and do all the wrong things. Think about it. Have you ever really liked someone and you wanted that person to like you, but each time you talked to him or her you said something foolish? You probably started trying to impress and stopped acting like yourself. It is the same in sport. When the competition is more important, you cannot change your performance or perform like someone else. You have to play your game well. You cannot immediately start hitting harder, taking shots you never made before, or maneuvering through five opponents when dribbling was not your strength. The problem is that the situation becomes so important to you that you will try everything and anything to get the outcome you want, when in fact, the best approach is just doing what you do best that day. And remember, you don't "have to," you "want to," and more importantly, you "can do."

Become the Athlete who Embraces the Pressure

The more exposure to and experience with high pressure situations, the better the typical response of an athlete. In other words, the more final second free throws you have to make and the more championship games you play in, the easier it is to embrace rather than fear these moments. However, it takes time to build up those experiences. Thus the purpose of this section is to help you handle and improve your performance in those situations today.

Many athletes think the response they first feel is their only possible response. They do not realize they can control and change their response and reaction to pressure. We continually ask athletes the following: "What does it feel like when you are nervous?" and "What does it feel like when you are excited?" After a few moments they usually get it. The physical responses to nervousness and excitement are practically the same. You get the butterflies in your stomach and your heart starts beating a bit faster. The difference is those who define it as negative get distracted by the feelings and think more negative thoughts, while the athletes who define it as excitement feel normal and ready once the competition starts. As an athlete, it is important for you to know how you respond in these situations and have tools to help you foster a more effective response. Therefore, it is important to work on the following:

- Identify Your Typical Response to Pressure
- Change Your Interpretation
- Focus on Your Game
- Let Go of Mistakes
- Learn to Relax

Identify Your Typical Response to Pressure

The key to controlling your thoughts and responses is first knowing them. Several techniques can be used to help you identify your response, including, but not limited to, journaling, asking a coach, videotaping practices and games, or having a parent or friend document specific scenarios (e.g., response after missing first serve). We, however, will focus on journaling because of its proven effectiveness and encouragement of personal accountability. You do not need to write a large amount of information to journal effectively. It is best to note your mindset before practice and competition. Write down what you did that morning, how you felt, how much sleep you got, etc. Write down important behaviors like eating, talking to friends, and worrying about a test. Following the competition or practice jot down your level of effectiveness. After a couple weeks, look through your notes and see if there are any trends. Were you more relaxed, focused, tense, or excited on some days than others? And, most importantly, did your mindset impact your performance? If you can identify what you were feeling and what influenced those feelings, you can recreate those situations in the future.

For example, a college track and field athlete started keeping a journal (with much hesitation) and ultimately discovered that he was putting excess pressure on himself before competitions, but staying loose and having fun before practices. This mindset resulted in successful practices, but poor performances during competition. In fact, he started thinking about competition the night before. He would not talk to anyone else because he believed he was getting focused. The day of competition he would review his races over and over again, not talking to teammates and maintaining a very serious attitude. Just prior to competition he would scout out his opponents, identify where they stood in the rankings and decide whether he could or could not beat them. In essence, he was deciding the outcome of his races before he even ran them. On the contrary, before practices he would hang out and stretch with his teammates, making jokes about who he was going to crush that day and challenge them to come after him. The result of this pre-practice routine was a relaxed and happy athlete who enjoyed competing. This athlete was two different people, fun and extroverted before practice and serious and introverted before competition. He realized this distinction negatively impacted his performance because being totally focused and serious also made him tense. Over time he created a more user-friendly pre-competition routine, which included joking around with teammates and focusing on himself and not his opponents.

The key to journaling is writing enough before and after the practice or competition to be able to identify a mindset and outcome relationship. You will not necessarily be able to identify or create a mindset that always leads to a win, but you will identify a mindset that is most likely to put you in the best position to perform well that day.

A golfer started journaling during her tournaments. She would jot down a few words following each hole. After the tournament she looked back over her notes and recognized that her written comments dictated how she felt on the next hole. Through the process of journaling she learned how she handled tough versus easy shots. She noticed she was putting pressure on herself to "make up" for a bad hole and she recognized this was negatively influencing her later shots. Over time she was able to mold her comments to help her translate the situation as a positive challenge as opposed to a negative pressure filled moment.

Athletes can choose to journal for as long or short a period of time as they need and like. Because it is useful for identifying trends, journaling can become a quick and easy habit that athletes use for years. Others, however, choose to journal for a few weeks, identify a trend and make a change.

Change Your Interpretation

The second step toward becoming an athlete who embraces pressure situations is changing your interpretation. Think about what happens inside your body and mind when coach says, "Get on the line." Some athletes tighten up, feel nervous and tell themselves they are not good at running. Others will get excited, knowing they are fast runners and this is a time for them to shine. The key is choosing words that can change your interpretation of the situation from negative to positive and from scary to exciting. You might not be the best runner, but this could be a good time to work on your conditioning or show improvements from the previous session. When you feel the butterflies, it is up to you to define them as "nervousness" or "readiness." A professional football player used to throw up before every game. You can imagine that many people would describe that as nerves. He translated it as a positive part of his pre-game routine (i.e., just getting rid of the garbage).

You have the power to use your words to create the feeling you want. The game is on the line. Do you want the ball? It is all in the interpretation. Do you call yourself "a gamer"? Do you tell yourself you thrive under pressure? Will you tell yourself, "I love these moments" or will you say, "I hope I don't miss"? What happens when your coach tells you in order to play, you MUST do well in the upcoming scrimmage or when your mother invites your entire extended family to your next meet? Are you excited, or do you feel nervous?

Similar to athletic competition, students often have to change their interpretation concerning schoolwork. Students get so overwhelmed by loads of reading, assignments and tests. They feel negative pressure to complete everything at once and often focus their thoughts on what they cannot do as opposed to what they can do. Again, we feel it is all in your mind, your focus and your interpretation. If you tell yourself you cannot complete the work, you never perform well in big competitions, or you choke when your coach is watching, your decision will be your outcome. However, if you practice changing your approach, by first changing your interpretation, you might just surprise yourself. The student must reinterpret the situation as "I can read one page at a time" and "I can complete one assignment at a time." He also can tell himself, "I love reading" and "I love a challenge." No, he cannot read five books at once or complete all assignments in one day, but he can do them one at a time.

The words you use to explain a situation can influence your mood and desire to engage in the moment. Rather than explaining the task as insurmountable, identify the part you can accomplish. Focus on what you can do and see it as a situation or assignment in which you can be successful. Start with some simple ones: "I love playing in the rain," "I thrive when the game gets close," "I'm glad you are here to see me do great things today," or "I'm at my best under pressure."

Focus on Your Game

Once you have reinterpreted the situation, you must shift your attention to your performance or your skills. Many teams and athletes spend far too much time before a competition focusing on what an opponent will do. They modify their game or play to match or counter opponents' strength, rather than spending the majority of time on their own strengths. Think about it. You have been honing your skills as an individual and forming your strategies as a team to make you the best. Therefore, this should be the focus. Yes, it is good to know if your opponent has a really strong forehand so you can give him more backhand shots or knowing that the goalie typically goes down so you should shoot high. Those are just smart tactics, but focusing only on opponents' strengths puts too much power in their hands. You need to approach all matches and competitions as if you are the fox, not the rabbit. You need to see yourself as the "hunter," not the one being "hunted."

Each game, competition, or challenge must be approached with the belief that you can be successful. By focusing on your strengths, skills, and game plan, you begin embracing the pressure. Coaches and athletes show fear by focusing more on their opponents than on themselves. It does not matter if you are playing the Los Angeles Lakers or the Bad News Bears. Your opponents should be nameless and faceless. Pressure is not elicited by the color of your opponents' uniforms or the names on their shirts. The pressure comes from your interpretations. Therefore, it is up to you to interpret the situation in your favor and stay focused on what you control, which is how you perform.

Let Go of Mistakes

Even athletes who focus on themselves and their performances can still fall victim to feeling the pressure. In fact, many times the pressure athletes feel is completely self-induced from an intense desire to perform perfectly. When a performance does not match an athlete's aspiration, the mistakes or failures are hard to accept. Often athletes turn on the pressure to perform better next time. If the next chance is not immediate, some athletes hold on to these thoughts for hours, days or even weeks. Internal pressure is not easy to handle and can be detrimental to future performances and current levels of confidence; therefore, athletes will benefit from first letting go of mistakes and then learning from them. Following are several possible strategies for letting go of mistakes. You may find some suggestions easier to adopt than others. The key is trying and practicing one or more of the approaches in order to identify what works best for you.

- Incorporate Reality Checks
- Adhere to the 3-Second Rule
- Recognize-Release-Focus Forward
- Use Post-Performance Shower to Let Go
- Keep a Journal

Incorporate Reality Checks

The first strategy for letting go of mistakes is called the "reality check." Once you recognize you made a mistake, quickly and objectively assess the situation. Remind yourself to be rational, not emotional. Use a simple key word or cue word to convince yourself it was just one mistake. For example, a male golfer took a shot, which he claimed was the "world's worst" shot. In his head he repeated this mantra over and over, ultimately ruining the remainder of the round. Upon reflection he realized that his statement was ridiculous and detrimental to his overall performance, when in fact, it was just one shot. In future situations he caught himself, and conducted a reality check. He would ask himself, "How bad was it?" He then more objectively answered the question. If it was bad, he would say, "Pretty bad, but still just one shot." If it was not really that horrible, he would say, "Not that bad. I can make a good shot from there." By taking the moment to check himself, he was able to be more objective, which kept his thoughts and comments more positive, leading him to feel less pressure and just compete.

Reality checks are great for helping you let go of any negative thought. Think about the last time your coach made you feel terrible. You probably replayed his words over and over and discussed what he did with your friends and teammates. After all the discussion, you likely felt even worse because what may have been a small event was now a big situation in your mind. You would have been better off conducting a reality check by first asking yourself, "What did coach actually say? Was it bad?" Then answer your own questions. For example, "Yes, it was that bad. He said I never do anything right." Finally follow up with, "What's the reality?" Now you have to be willing to remove emotions and think logically. For example, "Coach was angry and he was reacting emotionally." The key to an effective reality check is being rational in your response once you ask yourself the questions. Think of the most logical reason and stick with it.

Adhere to the 3-Second Rule

The 3-second rule concerns the amount of time you should allow yourself to think about a mistake. Give yourself no more than three seconds to deal with a mistake and then move on to the next play or sequence. By the time you make a bad pass in soccer and the opposing team throws the ball in, the mistake should be gone. As a wide receiver in football, by the time you drop a pass and get back to the huddle, the mistake should be dealt with and you should be ready to focus on the next play. The 3-second rule can apply to most sports but in some situations, you do not even have that long. The longer you linger on the negative, the more pressure you will feel to do better the next time. The harder you try to "do better," the worse you typically perform. Therefore, take three seconds and then move on!

Recognize-Release-Focus Forward

In addition to the previously mentioned strategies, this too helps athletes let go of mistakes. It works because you only have the capacity to think about one thought at a time. In other words, if you are thinking about a pink elephant, you cannot be simultaneously thinking about the ball you just missed. To help illustrate this point, think about a time you tried checking your e-mail while talking on the telephone. Do you know what your friend was saying or what you read in the e-mail? The likelihood is you had to say "what?" several times as your mind switched back and forth between the phone conversation and the e-mail. It is impossible to fully pay attention to both conversations (virtual and live) at the same time (regardless of how well you think you can multi-task). Your attention shifts back and forth from one conversation to the next and you pick up bits and pieces of both.

This same concept applies to athletic performances. If you are thinking about the mistake you just made, there is no way you are thinking about the current play. Therefore, first recognize the thoughts then release them. This can be done in a variety of ways. For example, a tennis player would recognize his thoughts, smile as his release and then say "ball" to focus his thoughts forward. The smile was the opposite of his natural response. He had to do it consciously, which encouraged him to purposefully behave rather than unconsciously react. This technique encourages you to recognize where your mind is before consciously redirecting your thoughts.

Similarly, you could use "thought stopping." This is a fairly simple technique that just requires practice. Before you try it, you need to have a replacement thought on your mind. This thought can be an image or a word (and to help relieve pressure it can be something that makes you laugh or smile). For example, a volleyball player had a tendency to focus on what she thought her coach was thinking, which left her second guessing her own actions and feeling extremely nervous while she played. She practiced recognizing those distracting thoughts. When they entered her mind she immediately pictured her male history teacher in a Speedo (apparently not a pretty picture). This visual would immediately distract her from thinking about her coach and make her smile. This momentary change in thinking allowed for an easy transition to the next step, which was to say her key word and focus forward on her play instead of backward on her coach. By intentionally breaking the thought, she took control of her mind and her performance.

You may think this is too simple so it could not work, but we challenge you to try it. Think about how quickly thoughts can change. You can be in the worst mood, ruminating over a fight with your parents, when your best friend comes in and tells you a joke. Immediately your thoughts switch from parents to joke. Similarly, have you ever been driving in the car when a sad song comes on the radio and you sing along, near tears thinking of an ex-boyfriend or girlfriend? Moments later your favorite party song starts playing and you are smiling and dancing to the beat with no residual memory of the previous moment. We have the capacity to switch our moods, emotions and thoughts very quickly, which is why it is possible to redirect your thoughts away from a mistake or pressure, and on to a useful, action-oriented thought.

Use Post-Performance Shower to Let Go

For those of you who have a difficult time letting go of entire games or poor performances long after the competition ended, the following strategy may be useful. A football player had a very hard time with this, leaving him angry sometimes for days. He was a very competitive athlete who took great pride in his effort and execution and he was not happy following a below standard performance. His personal frustration further impacted other performances and even his relationships outside football. After some trial and error with different techniques, he discovered an effective method. He would not allow himself to shower until he was ready to let go of the negative thoughts. Early on, there were times when he did not take a shower for a long time after a poor performance. Over time he realized brooding over a poor performance was not productive and the process helped him see how silly he was being. He now uses the water running over his head as a symbol of cleansing himself of a poor performance. He devises a plan to address areas of weakness in his game during the next practice or game and then leaves the locker room more relaxed.

Keep a Journal

As well as helping you learn about your response to pressure, journaling can provide you with an opportunity to minimize negative thoughts. This can be seen in the experience of Sarah Bullard, the youngest lacrosse player to ever make the National Team. She made the team as a sophomore in college. As with the other athletes, she has very high expectations of her performance. Sarah's method of "letting go" is to write in a journal. After each competition, she will write down aspects of her game she felt went poorly. She then writes down a few goals or strategies for how she will address those aspects of her game in the next practice or competition. The last words she writes reflect positive aspects of her performance. She recognizes this is critical for building confidence, releasing pressure and moving forward. In other words, she reflects, writes, plans and moves on.

The strategies taken as a whole encourage athletes to leave mistakes in the past and focus on the moment. By letting go of, and learning from, mistakes you are taking control and telling yourself you are capable of success. Regardless of the amount of pressure you initially feel, by letting go of mistakes, you minimize the amount of pressure you take with you. This allows you to feel better, perform better, and ultimately be successful in more pressure packed situations.

Learn to Relax

A final strategy for thriving in pressure situations is physically relaxing. As we mentioned, pressure evokes changes in blood pressure, heart rate, sweating and muscle tension, to name a few. In order for you to feel more calm, cool and collected, you can practice deep breathing and progressive muscle relaxation.

Deep Breathing

When you encounter a stressor, your body prepares to fight or run away, leading to an increase in breathing, blood pressure, etc. This physical response may negatively influence or distract your thinking and physically exhaust your body, leading to poor performance. Therefore, the first and easiest response to a stressful or pressure packed situation is taking a deep breath. This helps you slow your body's responses and regain control.

A deep breath involves inhaling as much air as possible and then slowly releasing the air from your lungs. Try it right now. Inhale as much air as you can while counting to three. Once your chest is full, slowly release the air and allow all of it to leave your body. You should feel your shoulders drop, your muscles relax and an overall more loose feeling. This technique is beneficial because it is easy and it can be done anywhere. Perhaps your coach just pulled you aside and said, "Look. The competition is going to come down to your performance today. I want to see your best stuff." At that moment you might feel like the weight of the world is on your shoulders. Walk away, take a few seconds and take two deep breaths. You should be able to regain your composure and direct your thoughts forward to what you want to do and how you will bring your "A" game today.

Progressive Muscle Relaxation

Similar to the deep breath, progressive muscle relaxation also helps you modify your physical reaction to pressure. This technique leads to greater awareness of muscle tension and relaxation. Prior to competing it is important for your muscles to be primed and ready, but not too tight. Similarly, you do not want to be too loose as that could be a sign of complacence or disinterest. Therefore, it is important to know your body and recognize optimal muscle tension for performance.

Progressive muscle relaxation requires the athlete to tense and relax each muscle group independently. Typically athletes start with the muscles in their feet and end with the muscles in their face. By physically tightening and then relaxing the muscles on your own, you better learn how they feel in both of those states. Try it now. Squeeze your hands into a tight fist and feel the tension for five seconds. After five seconds, slowly release your hands and allow them to drop. Now, leaving your hands loose, bend your arms and tighten your biceps for five seconds. Again, slowly release the muscle and allow your arms to fall by your side. You would do this with all muscle groups until your body is totally relaxed. You should practice this technique during the week to become better aware of, and in more control of, your muscles.

This technique often is used to help athletes get to bed at night or as a means of relaxing the body after competition. It is also useful the night before competition to engage in progressive muscle relaxation followed by an imagery session. Individuals more experienced with this technique also modify it to use during the day of, or prior to, competition by only tensing and releasing specific muscles. For example, many people tighten their shoulders and neck when they are nervous. Instead of leaving those muscles tight and starting your competition tense, it would be beneficial to quickly tighten and relax them to get your body to an ideal pre-competitive state. Try it now. Squeeze your shoulders up to your ears for five seconds. Feel the discomfort before slowly letting them fall, releasing all built up tension. You will loosen the muscles and feel more relaxed and ready to compete. It is important to note you would never want to engage in a full progressive muscle relaxation prior to competition as you would be more ready for bed than high level performance.

You know that stressors will never completely disappear as sport in general, and the life of an athlete, is full of "pressures." However, hopefully you have learned some techniques and strategies to help you translate and handle those moments more effectively. Great athletes experience pressure, but they thrive in those moments because they have learned how to interpret them in their favor. With practice, hopefully you will join the ranks of the "great."

Key Points to Remember

1. It is all about interpretation: If you define the situation as overwhelming, you will feel overwhelmed.

2. There is no difference in the skills you must execute in the first minutes of play or the final seconds of regulation.

3. The skills you practiced to get you to the "big game" are the same skills you will need to execute at the "big game." Although the crowd may be bigger and the venue more impressive, the game does not change.

4. You can control how you think about the competition and you can control how your mind and body respond.

5. Before you can change how you react to pressure, you first must identify how you respond. Start journaling to identify trends in behaviors and thoughts.

6. Sometimes you just need to smile and take a deep breath.

7. Take a moment to review your answers to the questions at the beginning of the chapter. What changes can you make to help you embrace pressure?

Demonstrate Positive Character

*Any guy who can maintain a positive attitude
without much playing time certainly earns my
respect.*
EARVIN "MAGIC" JOHNSON

*I am still determined to be cheerful and happy,
in whatever situation I may be; for I have also
learned from experience that the greater part
of our happiness or misery depends upon our
dispositions, and not upon our circumstances.*
MARTHA WASHINGTON

Think About It

Take a moment to begin examining your character by answering the following questions:

How do you handle adversity?

Do you demonstrate a positive attitude and effort regardless the role you play on your team?

Would others say you are a good teammate to be around every day?

Are you willing to cheat to win?

Would you take a "magic pill" if it meant you could be the best in your sport?

Do you respect your sport and your opponents enough to compete with class?

Some people believe that participating in sport helps create positive character traits, while others claim sport merely reveals your existing character. Ultimately it probably does both. With the right coaching and personal dedication, athletes have the opportunity to develop admirable qualities through sport that will benefit them for the rest of their lives. The characteristics people hope sport develops include: (a) discipline, (b) work ethic, (c) loyalty and (d) perseverance, to name a few. However, it is obvious when looking at any team to see that not all athletes possess these attributes. Therefore, they must be fostered by coaches, parents and, most importantly, they must be worked on by athletes themselves.

It is also important to point out that unless you have parents or coaches who emphasize it, your moral character will not be developed just because you are an athlete. Think about all the athletes who have gotten caught over the years. Whether their problems involve altering equipment or taking steroids, the reality is not all athletes take the moral high road. We have seen athletes lie and cheat. Athletes have been caught screaming at referees or talking bad about teammates. Some athletes are great at handling minor setbacks and others show their true colors when situations do not go their way. What about you? Do you lie, cheat or steal in any way to increase your chances of winning? Have you ever called a ball out in tennis when you knew it hit the line? Would you take a questionable substance if you knew it would make you faster? Would you do fewer repetitions in the weight room if you knew no one was watching? Your response to these questions says a great deal about your character.

The next few pages are dedicated to helping you examine and perhaps improve aspects of your character that will help you become a better athlete and person. We will focus the discussion around handling adversity, competing with class, and leaving a positive legacy. You also will be provided with strategies to help improve all of these areas. It is important to be honest with yourself as you read the next few pages and be willing to make changes if needed.

Handling Adversity

Adversity in sport can include a variety of situations on or off the field. Sometimes the situation is minor such as a bad call by an official or bad weather on competition day. Other situations are more severe, like experiencing an injury or playing a role you dislike all season. Regardless of the source of adversity, your character will dictate your response. Following we will discuss: (a) how you can handle minor setbacks while demonstrating positive character, (b) the influence of body language, (c) responding to injury, and (d) making the most of your role on a team.

Handling Minor Setbacks

What is your response when an official makes a call you feel is wrong? How do you respond when the weather is not ideal? Do you show your frustration when things are not going your way? Do you make a scene or claim they are "out to get you"? Do you hang your head, stomp your feet or roll your eyes? Do you get so frustrated that you let it affect you for several minutes after it occurs? Does your reaction negatively influence others? If you answered "yes" to any of these questions, it is important to change your response.

The most important concept to understand regarding officials, bad weather, or other minor setbacks is you have no control over them. Therefore you must learn to deal with these issues and move on. Any of the strategies already discussed for letting go of mistakes (e.g., the 3-second rule, reality checks, or recognize-release-focus forward) also could be used to effectively deal with these situations.

It takes a more resilient athlete to handle a bad call and move on than to argue or make a scene. For example, one of the most talented athletes on a college field hockey team had a very difficult time letting go of these calls. She would get angry, show her frustration and spend at least 10 seconds post-call complaining. Of course, play did not stop in these moments, leaving her opponent with a huge advantage during her outbursts. This response was selfish as it left her teammates one athlete down. Challenge yourself to be the mentally tough athlete in these situations and leave it up to your coaches to deal with officials. To do this effectively and not waste time dwelling on what you cannot change, sometimes you'll have to swallow your pride or bite your tongue. Although this may not be your "initial" reaction, it can be your "trained" response.

Let's face it; we all know that everything does not always go the way we planned. Rain falls when you do not want it and buses break down before major tournaments. Just as you previously imagined yourself being successful in ideal situations, you should also imagine yourself responding effectively to negative situations before they happen. Imagine yourself responding appropriately to the bad call, playing through bad weather or positively handling any adversity that typically causes you trouble. Imagine yourself responding in a way you would want others to respond. Develop a plan that includes behaviors and responses to best handle these situations so they do not negatively impact your performance.

Perhaps you are a wide receiver in football who does not like to compete when it is cold outside or you are a tennis player who struggles in windy conditions. You should imagine yourself handling these difficult situations as a mentally tough athlete who does not allow weather to affect your mentality. Imagine yourself reading the conditions and modifying your swing accordingly. You can imagine yourself receiving the football with soft hands on a cold night. Perhaps you have gotten frustrated in the past when you or your team was losing at half time. Again, imagine yourself responding in a mentally tough way. If you take the time to imagine these scenarios in advance, you are less likely to be taken by surprise when they actually happen. You also are more likely to respond effectively because you already have a plan and you have seen yourself carrying it out.

Your planned behavior may include a deep breath, a cue word to switch your focus, or snapping a rubber band on your wrist as a personal reminder to move on. Athletes with positive character will practice this in advance so they do not just react emotionally to the situation. Instead, when adversity strikes they are prepared to respond positively and effectively. You cannot prepare for, or know, everything that may happen, but you can prepare yourself to better handle adverse situations as a whole.

Demonstrate Positive Body Language

When athletes do not practice or prepare for adverse situations they often get caught up in the emotion and just react. The reaction is often negative and generally obvious to outsiders. When athletes respond based on emotion, they typically demonstrate poor body language. By hanging your head, frowning, or looking to the sky with a questioning and frustrated gaze, you are basically admitting defeat. This response can be very distracting for teammates, while simultaneously providing strength to your opponent. Remember, if your opponents know you are struggling, it will lift their spirits and give them the confidence and belief that they have an edge.

Angel McCoughtry, a First Team All-American Forward for the University of Louisville Women's Basketball Team and the first pick in the 2009 WNBA draft, admits that she used to regularly display negative body language. She had no idea her body language was so negative until her coach showed a series of video clips of her responding after mistakes or when things were not going well. She was shocked at her own reactions.

She made a commitment from that day to change her body language because she knew it affected her confidence, focus, and her team.

Do you show your frustration or anger on your face and body? Have someone film you for several competitions and/or practices. Then watch the video to see what type of body language you demonstrate after mistakes, during practice or when receiving feedback. You might be surprised by what you see. Later you can practice picking your head up, standing straight and acting assertively. You can practice maintaining eye contact when coach provides feedback or saying "thanks" when a teammate tries to help. Practice using your body language to improve your game, as opposed to letting it hurt your performance. Work on body language that earns you respect rather than contempt from peers, coaches, and referees.

Handling Major Setbacks

Injury

If you participate in sport long enough, there is a chance you might be seriously injured. Being injured is not only a test of your physical fortitude, but it can be a test of your character and attitude as well. Your response to injury, if it does happen, is critical to a speedy recovery. It has been shown that many athletes respond to injury much like someone might respond to the death of a close loved one. The typical stages (adapted from Kubler-Ross, 1969) include:

1. Disbelief, Denial and Isolation
2. Anger directed at themselves and others
3. Depression over the fact that normal comfort, freedom, and opportunity are gone
4. Acceptance of and/or resignation to the situation and ideally a commitment to follow the rehabilitation protocol

While these thoughts and feelings about an injury are normal and part of the rehabilitation process for most injured athletes, it does not mean they are ideal for positively handling the situation. Therefore, it is imperative to understand you have a choice in how you respond to both your injury and your rehabilitation. This is a situation where your emotional maturity will make a difference. The way you think about your injury and the behaviors you employ will dictate your success in recovery and satisfaction during the process.

Athletes who remain in the Disbelief, Anger or Depression stages will continue to focus on the negatives. Often these athletes respond negatively to teammates, coaches, family and friends. They will reveal weakness by focusing on what they cannot do, why the situation is not fair or how they are not being supported. On the other hand, the mentally tough athlete will reveal strength of character. She will work on her rehab so she can return to her team and competition. He will find ways to get what he needs to be successful, whether it is more ice from the athletic trainer, a job from the coach or a word of support from a friend. It is important to remember that handling injury is difficult. Athletes often feel isolated, frustrated and scared of what is to come. But, the fact is you cannot undo the past and you cannot dictate the outcome; all you can do is control how you think about your situation and what you do to make the best of your time.

You Get What You Give

Athletes have told us they are treated differently by teammates and coaches during their time as injured athletes. Coaches have explained this often happens because they do not know what to do or say around people with injuries. They do not know if they should discuss competition or ask how you feel, which many times results in no discussion at all. As well, coaches and teammates recognize their job must go on. With or without you, they have to prepare and compete. This may sound harsh, but put yourself in their shoes. You may be right to feel neglected, but you have the power to hang your head and sulk in the training room or step out and do what you can with your coach and your team. You can help coaches and teammates feel more comfortable around you by telling them what is going on and asking them for what you need. In addition, remember you often get what you give. Negative athletes during injury tend to get less attention and support compared to positive athletes. So, ask yourself honestly: are they neglecting me or am I pulling away from them?

Accept It

The goal of all injured athletes should be to reach the Acceptance stage as quickly as possible. Only then will you truly commit to your rehabilitation program and possess the proper mindset and attitude to move forward. To help facilitate your recovery, you should incorporate several of the techniques that have been discussed in previous sections. Set outcome, performance and daily process goals so that you can actually chart your improvements. Setting goals such as attending and being on time to each rehab session and improving your range of motion by a certain percentage each day will help you stay focused on getting healthy. Of course, prepare yourself for setbacks along the way. In fact, it might be beneficial to include mental toughness goals on days the physical part of the rehab is difficult. For example, "I will eliminate negative comments during rehab today" or "I won't complain about my injury." And hardest of all may be those days you cannot do anything physical. On those days set goals concerning interactions with teammates, helping your coach, or try focusing on school.

Additionally, use the imagery skills you have developed to imagine the injury healing at a faster rate and becoming stronger than it was before. You also can imagine yourself making a successful return to competition. Practice seeing yourself performing with confidence instead of looking timid and favoring your injury. Finally, you can coach yourself up by changing negative thoughts such as, "This isn't fair" or "Rehab hurts too much" to more helpful thoughts like, "I can't control that I got injured, but I can control how I respond" or "Even though it hurts, this is helping me get back."

Find Support

Surrounding yourself with people who care about you and are supportive also can help you stay positive during the process. These people are integral to how you handle this process because they will be there for you when you need to vent your frustrations or to remind you to stick to your rehab. Beware of those who bring you down or allow you to wallow too long. Strength of character when handling injury does not mean you never get upset, but it does mean you do not dwell on it. You need positive people who help you focus on what you can do and what you can control. Make sure you spend as much of your time as possible with these people during the process.

Be Patient

Last but certainly not least, you must be patient. Competitive and dedicated athletes who are passionate about their sport want to get back to competition as soon as they can. Unfortunately, some athletes push the rehab process at an unhealthy pace and come back too soon. It is important to listen to your trainers and doctors and follow their protocol for your recovery. The worst possible outcome is going back too early, injuring yourself again and then being out of competition even longer than originally planned. Pushing to return too quickly may show work ethic, but it does not show discipline or loyalty because you likely will be more of a deficit than a benefit to your team when you return still injured.

Overall, use your time wisely and do periodic "attitude checks." Are you helping your teammates from the sidelines? Are you doing what you can to heal? Are you asking your coach what you can do to be a productive member of the team? Or, are you the "downer" on the team, frustrated by your injury and annoyed that others just do not understand? Injuries are tough. Allow yourself to vent, but then focus forward and find a way to make the most of what you can do today.

Not Playing the Role You Want

Another area that provides a very clear picture of athletes' character is how they handle their role. Any competitor wants the chance to compete. Unless you are a starter or play most of the time, there is a chance you are not happy with your role. We are not saying that you should be satisfied. It is never bad to want more. However, you have to recognize the role you have, why you have it, and do your best in that position until you earn a different role. Otherwise stated, you have to embrace your role because your behaviors and comments during these times reveal a great deal about your character. Following are suggestions for how you can make the most of your time in any role, while revealing a positive character and working to earn the position you desire. They include:

- Avoid Complaining
- Support Your Teammates Regardless of Your Role
- Be a Sail, Not an Anchor
- Focus on Attitude and Effort

Avoid Complaining

Negative character is revealed in athletes who complain about their role because these athletes typically talk bad about their coach and the athlete in their desired position. We hear it all the time. "Coach made the wrong decision" and "That athlete isn't better than me." It is one thing to have these thoughts and share them with your roommate or best friend when no one else is around. It is totally different if you make your unhappiness widely known. This is not the response of a good teammate and it reveals a great deal about your character.

Regardless of your current role, it is important to embrace it while working and developing your skills so you may one day change that role. Complaining keeps your focus on the problem, not the solution. As well, you should be careful to whom you complain. Many athletes grumble to parents, who often intensify athletes' frustrations. This happens when they agree with their sons and daughters while attempting to be supportive. As much as they might try, it is difficult for parents to be objective and look at the situation from others' perspectives when it comes to playing time for their children.

Therefore, instead of talking to your teammates and/or your parents about playing time, why not take a solution focused approach and talk to your coach. Ask him or her to provide you with specific aspects of your performance that you need to work on and then it is your job to commit to improving those areas. Keep in mind there are no guarantees for more playing time or a different role just because you improve in these areas. It just means you are doing what you can to put yourself in the best position to succeed and perhaps influence your coach's decision. More importantly, you are building mental toughness and other qualities demonstrating a positive character.

Support Your Teammates Regardless of Your Role

You also can display positive character from your position on the bench during competition. When you are not competing, your job is to cheer and support your teammates. What message do you send your teammates on and off the field if you isolate yourself or hang your head because you are not playing the role you want? Similarly, what message do you send when the entire team is celebrating after a hard fought win and you refuse to join because you barely played? In both scenarios, you are sending a very strong message that it is really about you and not the team. You are more important than the team. Do you really want to send that type of message?

One particular athlete explained her frustration over sitting on the sidelines watching the team play. She explained "their" successes and "their" losses, feeling no connection because of her role. After a season of watching and feeling like she did not belong, she realized how her attitude and perspective were ruining her experience and her relationship with teammates and coaches. Remember, you get what you give. If you act negatively, you will attract similar responses from others.

Be a Sail, Not an Anchor

Every team can be described as a ship sailing to its destination. As a member of that team, you are either a sail helping that ship reach its target or an anchor holding it back. If you are talking bad about the coach or the athlete in front of you on the depth chart and pouting because you are not getting the playing time you want, then you are an anchor undermining the potential success of your team. If you are a positive addition to the team, providing those intangibles coaches always talk about, you are a sail. Which are you—the anchor or the sail?

It is much easier to be a sail when everything is going your way. If you play all the time or have your ideal role, you really have no excuse for not being a sail. Think about your teammates who do not get to play, yet practice day after day with the goal of making you better. Think about your teammates who work hard every day bringing their positive attitude and other qualities to the team environment. It is important to acknowledge these teammates and let them know how much you respect them and their contributions. This does not have to be a public acknowledgement. You can do it on the way back to the locker room, after practice or at least in a text message. These people are clearly the main sails for your team and they make a significant and often overlooked contribution. Positive character is reflected in how one handles both adversity and success. As a successful athlete, do you recognize when someone else needs a lift?

Focus on Attitude and Effort

As we have pointed out, most competitive athletes want playing time. One additional factor you should consider when fretting over playing time is how much control you actually have over it. In reality, you have no control. You can influence it, but you ultimately do not control it. You are not the one who writes the names on the official line-up card. You cannot go to coach and say, "Coach, I know I haven't started all season, but I have been working very hard and I looked better than the girl in front of me this week, so go ahead and put me down as the starter today and let me play." Your coach is ultimately in control of who plays. We consult with many athletes who spend an inordinate amount of time worrying about their playing time even though it is not something they can control. We challenge them to turn their focus away from playing time and on to the two factors they completely control, namely, attitude and effort.

There is no correlation between your talent level and your attitude and effort. In other words, whether you are the most talented athlete or the least talented athlete on your team, you can demonstrate a great attitude and effort each day. There are several examples of very talented athletes who have led by example in terms of their attitude and effort. Michael Jordan was legendary for his work ethic. Regardless of how many points he scored each game, Jordan would shoot extra before and after practice. He was the hardest worker on his team and he challenged his teammates to match his efforts. Kobe Bryant is the same way today in his role with the Los Angeles Lakers, as is Peyton Manning with the Indianapolis Colts and Derek Jeter of the New York Yankees. Dara Torres, the Olympic swimmer, and Mia Hamm, the international soccer star, are also exceptionally gifted athletes who set a standard for teammates and competitors in terms of attitude and effort. They were and are known as much for their work ethic as their athletic prowess. Athletes such as these could take days off and coast, but they want to be the best, so they work harder than the others. They knew and know that to be the best, you have to work when others are not. Whether you are the most talented or least talented athlete on the team, you always can set yourself apart as a leader through your attitude and effort. People may respect you for your talent, but they will remember you for your extraordinary work ethic and positive attitude.

While you have certainly heard of Michael Jordan, Kobe Bryant, Peyton Manning, Derek Jeter, Dara Torres and Mia Hamm, you probably have never heard of Josh Pastner. Josh was a freshman walk-on basketball player with the Arizona Wildcats the last time they won a national championship in 1997. Josh played only when the team was far ahead and he scored very few points throughout the year. However, "the kid who never played" was an integral part of the team. He would stay after practice and rebound for starters. He would ask the coaches if he could watch game film to see if he could find something that would help his team be successful for upcoming games. He wanted to do anything he could to help his team succeed. His team won a national championship that year and Josh Pastner was singled out as a major reason for their success. His teammates and coaches acknowledged they could not have done it without him. He was given a scholarship the next season and went on to become an assistant coach for the team after graduation. Josh is now head coach at the University of Memphis (Janssen, 1999).

Four former Duke athletes, Joe Kelly and Matt White from

Men's Soccer, Abigail Meyer from Women's Lacrosse and Greg Paulus from Men's Basketball, demonstrated exceptional attitude and effort throughout the ups and downs of their athletic careers. Matt and Joe had the opportunity to play significant minutes their first three years on the team and were both elected captains the spring of their junior years. As senior captains they expected to start and play significant minutes. However, the soccer program recruited a very talented freshman class and soon Joe and Matt found themselves playing very little. As you might imagine, they struggled with their demotion in playing time early in the season. But, very soon they made up their minds to do what was needed to positively influence the team. They worked very hard in practice, never publicly complaining about their roles or playing time. Matt and Joe's young teammates respected them and were willing to follow them throughout that season, never thinking these athletes were not leadership worthy because they did not start. That team won the Atlantic Coast Conference Tournament Championship and advanced through the playoffs to the College Cup which is comprised of the final four teams. They exceeded many expectations and Joe and Matt were a large reason for their success. These athletes easily could have become anchors and held the team back, but they chose to embrace their roles and lead by example.

Abigail Meyer worked very hard but never played significant minutes as a lacrosse player during her first two years at Duke. However, her hard work paid off her junior year when she earned a starting position. Abigail even started in the conference championship game against arch rival, the University of North Carolina. She felt very good about her performance and was excited about her senior year. Largely because of her work ethic and positive attitude, she was voted captain for her final year. However, due to an injury early in the season, Abigail lost her starting position and had a tough time earning that position back. She privately struggled with not playing but maintained her positive attitude on the field so as not to negatively influence her teammates. Abigail chose the high road and made her team better through her attitude and effort. Rather than expending negative energy complaining about the situation, she focused on doing all she could to help her team from her position. She was the one cheering the loudest and encouraging teammates frustrated with their performances or playing time. She made a huge difference on her team in ways that did not show up on the score board or in the stats sheets.

Greg Paulus, similar to the other three athletes, lost his starting position his senior year. He was a captain as a sophomore and he continued to start and play significant minutes his junior year. However, because of a unique team situation, he was not named captain that year. Greg was then elected captain again as a senior and although he started at the beginning of the season, he later lost his starting role. Throughout his ups and downs, Greg was an incredible leader and positive influence on his team. Any frustrations with his situation were not shared with many people. He chose to make a positive impact on his teammates on and off the court. You could see him on the bench during games cheering his teammates on and providing feedback to them during timeouts. He also was there for his teammates when they struggled. It is interesting to note that when the Duke Men's Basketball team won the 2009 ACC Tournament, Greg Paulus was the first guy off of the bench to run and find teammate Nolan Smith to celebrate. This is interesting because Nolan is the guy who was playing in Greg's position, which speaks volumes of Greg's character. He was most definitely a sail!

Each of the athletes described in this section are true champions not only because they are talented and work hard, but also because of their character. They all had choices as to how they were going to respond to a less than ideal situation. They could have complained about their situation and become anchors on their teams. Instead, they chose the response that highlights the high quality of their character. We all can learn a great deal from these and other athletes like them. Whatever your role, make the best of it. Do not complain about it, instead embrace it and fill it better than anyone else you know. Be an All-Conference, All-State or All-American performer in that role, but most importantly do it with class.

Compete With Class

Are you willing to do whatever it takes to win? Would you cheat in order to win? There are many examples in the media of athletes who value winning more than honesty or integrity. Numerous professional baseball and football players have admitted to taking steroids and Human Growth Hormone because it helped them perform better, recover faster, and in general gave them an edge over their competitors. The world of professional cycling has a long history of cyclists participating in illegal activities such as blood doping (re-infusing your own blood to increase the body's ability to carry oxygen) and using performance enhancing drugs. Even athletes at the college and high school levels demonstrate that winning is ultimately more important than playing the game the right way by committing some of the same violations as their professional counterparts. Several states including Florida, Texas and New Jersey have instituted drug testing at the high school level because this type of cheating has become so rampant.

Obviously, there are many other ways you can gain an unfair advantage on your opponents. Some athletes alter their equipment, lie regarding their age or legal place of residence, while some go as far as purposely injuring their opponents so they will not be able to compete. Regardless of the method, it is all cheating. It is difficult to understand why athletes cannot simply prepare themselves fully and then compete to see who is best, but cheating practices are not new in the sporting arenas. Evidence of such practices dates all the way back to Ancient Rome when Emperor Commodus would have animals and gladiators drugged prior to fighting them. It was said that he killed thousands of wild animals and people, proving his strength and skill, when in fact, these animals and people were already near death before the fight began. This might sound extreme and not relevant today, but even recently we have heard of athletes injuring their competitors or teammates to ensure a spot on the roster or a chance of success.

Why do some athletes go to such great lengths to gain an unfair advantage? Russell Gough (1997) says athletes often rationalize that it is okay to cheat because "everyone else is doing it." Therefore, cheating is the only way they can compete. Gough argues that we do not cheat because "everyone else is doing it." We cheat because of something we want. We want to win. We want the fame, money or college scholarship that goes along with winning and we value these perks over competing with class. Do you value winning over competing with class or is competing the right way important to you?

At the end of the day, you have to be able to look at yourself in the mirror and know that you competed with class. At some point the victories will lose their worth and the trophies will lose their luster. All you will have left is your character. So, do not get so caught up in having to win that you are willing to sacrifice your character. Do not let the fact that "everyone else is doing it" be an excuse to lure you into thinking you have to follow them. The truth is that everyone is not doing it. Such a thought merely provides a self-protective excuse for giving in to temptation. Winning should never be more important than competing with integrity.

Leave a Positive Legacy

Your values influence your behaviors and your behaviors influence your legacy. We all leave a legacy behind. Therefore, it is not a matter of **if** you will be remembered by your teammates, coaches and opponents; it is a matter of **how** you will be remembered. In his book *The 7 Habits of Highly Effective People*, Stephen Covey discusses the importance of "beginning with the end in mind." A person should think about what his life or career will look like upon retirement. You should use the same approach to your athletic career. Come up with characteristics or traits you want your teammates, coaches and opponents to say you exhibited throughout your career. You might use terms and phrases such as *hard worker, great attitude, cared more about the team than individual statistics, tough, relentless*, or *competed with class*, etc. These are what you hope people will say about you one, two, or three years down the road. Keep in mind they will not remember those qualities later if you are not behaving that way today. Therefore, a more important question is what would your teammates, coaches and opponents say if we were to ask them to describe you today?

Take a minute to write down the qualities you truly want to be remembered for by these three groups and place it somewhere you can see it regularly. Then ask yourself if you are living up to your desired legacy on a daily basis. What are you doing to make others believe you are the words on your wall? Also remember when creating your legacy that you will be remembered as much for the type of teammate and person you were as your athletic prowess. Therefore, although being the best hitter or the most aggressive defender is important, we also want you to add qualities related to you as a person. When creating your legacy, think about additional reasons your teammates are better off for having you on their team. Are you responsible, trustworthy, accountable and positive? Do your behaviors on and off the field earn the respect of others? The key to being the best athlete is also being the best person.

Key Points to Remember

1. Your character will be revealed in the way you handle adversity that comes your way.

2. Remember, you cannot control your playing time. However, you can control your attitude and effort.

3. Choose to be a sail, not an anchor.

4. Compete with class. No victory is worth it if you had to cheat to gain it.

5. You **will** leave a legacy with your teammates, coaches and opponents. Make sure it is one you are proud to leave behind.

6. Take a moment to review your answers to the questions at the beginning of the chapter. What changes can you make to improve your character?

Enjoy the Journey

*Do you know what my favorite part of
the game is? The opportunity to play.*
MIKE SINGLETARY

*If you worried about falling off the bike,
you'd never get on.*
LANCE ARMSTRONG

Think About it

Take a moment to begin examining your level of sport enjoyment by answering the following questions:

Why did you start participating in your sport?

Do you ever question why you still participate in sports?

Do parents, coaches or others influence how much or how little you enjoy your sport?

Are you able to enjoy an ugly win?

What is it that you love about your sport today?

To effectively maximize your athletic potential, you must recognize that your athletic career is going to pass very quickly. This happens when athletes forget why they began participating, focus only on the negatives, and lose their passion for the sport. Whether you are an athlete who pushes too hard, focuses on what is not good, or just goes through the daily motions, the outcome will be the same. You will end up looking back and thinking, "What if . . . ?"

Numerous athletes we have consulted with over the past several years have clearly lost their "love for the game." This includes college and professional athletes and sadly even high school athletes. Not only have they lost their love for the game, but the experience starts to feel like a "job." Many college athletes have admitted they would not compete if they were not receiving scholarship money.

What about you? Have you lost your passion and love for your sport or do you still have the same childlike enthusiasm you had when you first started competing? Do you look forward to going to most practice sessions or do you dread the multiple hour blocks of time? Do you still get excited about the possibilities of competing or do you fear not playing well or not playing at all?

Losing Passion

There are several internal and external factors that contribute to athletes losing their love for their sport. In particular, coaches who rely too heavily on coercion and fear to motivate athletes often affect a person's passion. Parents who live vicariously through their children and put unreasonable expectations or demands on performance can influence an athlete's love of the game. The constant barrage of media and "fair weather fans" can take a huge toll on one's enjoyment. In addition, the daily time, physical demands, and perceived pressures of the sport can play a role in minimizing one's enjoyment over the years.

As an athlete, it is important to realize you cannot always control how coaches, parents, the media and fans act. However, you can control how much you allow them to affect you and how you define your sport experience. As was discussed in the Embracing the Pressure section, you have control over how you respond to the situation. Athletes will often say, "Coach really causes me not to love this game," "My parents need to leave me alone because they are really making me hate my sport," or "The media really takes the fun away from being an athlete." It is important to realize that outside forces do not **cause** you to lose your love and passion for your sport. You **allow** them to sway your thinking. And, although it is not always easy to block out influences such as parents, coaches and negative media, it is possible. They may make comments or add stressors, but you do not have to accept them.

A college football player became frustrated with his sport, team and coaches. He came to practices angry, only heard negative comments from coaches, and constantly compared himself to the teammates playing in front of him. The athlete believed everyone was against him and he could not get a fair chance. Because of this he did not enjoy the season. Rather than focusing on what he could do in his role, making positive changes to his play and behavior, or communicating with his coach, the athlete chose to feel sorry for himself and blame his coach. It is not always easy identifying this downward spiral when you are in it. Therefore, it is crucial to take a step back and attempt to see the situation from the vantage point of others (e.g., coaches, teammates). Had this athlete taken a step back and allowed himself to momentarily relinquish his own beliefs, he would have seen that coach was not against him. In truth, the coach was merely playing the team he felt would best achieve their goals. Had this athlete taken time to think about the team and not just himself, he would have been better able to make some changes to his behaviors and his performance to help the cause and actually enjoy being a part of the team. He had forgotten one of the main reasons he was playing, specifically, the love of the game.

Remember Why You Participate

Take a minute to remind yourself why you started competing in your sport. Remind yourself how you used to feel on the way to the field, pool, track or course. Next, think about why you participate now. Finally, take a moment to deliberate on what you hope to achieve and why you hope to achieve that goal. If you do not know the answers to these questions, you likely are not that passionate about your sport or not that sure of yourself as an athlete. In either case, you will be more influenced by what others say and do. The stronger you feel about your sport and your purpose as an athlete, the easier it is to stay focused on the task, ignore externals and have fun in the process.

Reminding yourself why you started participating helps you focus on the positives, block out externals and replace negative, internal thoughts. Instead of hearing "why didn't you play more," or "you have a lot to improve," over and over, you can focus on "I love this game," "running fast makes me happy," or "I love the sound of the bat hitting the ball." Back when you started it was not all about winning or earning more playing time than your teammate. You used to participate because you loved trying, learning and practicing. You loved being with your friends, having fun, and improving.

So often athletes lose their passion as they rise in the ranks of their sport because competition gets tougher and they are no longer the best. This creates a whole new focus. Instead of just competing and loving the sport, their mission becomes gaining more playing time or beating someone else. This mindset leads to frustration, aggravation and sometimes even burnout. Therefore, to maintain the passion athletes must:

- View Your Sport as a Sanctuary
- Be Willing to Fail
- Have Fun
- Find What You Enjoy
- Enjoy All Wins—Even the Ugly Ones

View Your Sport as a Sanctuary

A strategy for changing your perception of your sport experience, and enjoying the journey, involves changing your mindset for practice or competition. View practice and competition as your time away from the outside world. See the field, pool, track or course as your "sanctuary" that no one can infiltrate. Adopt the attitude that no matter what others say or do, they cannot take away the fun and passion you have for your sport.

For example, Rachel Moss, an All-American volleyball player, took a moment prior to practice and viewed the volleyball court as her "sandbox." By seeing the court as a place where she used to play as a child, she was able to relax and enjoy the experience from the start. She basically was telling herself it's time to "play" like she did as a little girl. This strategy helped her escape the demands and pressures of the world outside as she entered her own personal playground.

Be Willing to Fail

Previously we discussed how your perspective on pressure impacts performance. Here we want to point out the influence on satisfaction. If you only perceive success as being number one, you are likely to lose your passion. If you fear the challenge of tough competition, you will never enjoy the games, and if you are afraid to lose, you will never be great. Winston Churchill said it best: "Success is not final, failure is not fatal: it is the courage to continue that counts." Sport is about picking yourself back up after a heartbreaking loss. It is about coming back to defend a hard won competition. If there was no challenge, it would not be as much fun to win. Think about it. How do you feel after beating your kid brother in a foot race or out shooting your four-foot-tall cousin? It is definitely not as fulfilling as out-touching your high school rival in the state swim meet or sinking the buzzer beater against the 3-time national champions.

Nobody likes losing and nobody goes in to fail, but it is a huge part of sport. Only one person wins the race and only one team ends their season with a "W." In 2003, Annika Sorenstam, arguably the best women's golfer in the world, took on the challenge of competing against men in the PGA. After missing the cut in the second round, she explained her purpose was to test herself. Her loss did not ruin her reputation, confidence, or place in golf history. In fact, being willing to stick her neck out made her even more memorable and perhaps more successful in her career. She needed that challenge to keep her passion alive and though she did not make it far in the tournament, she was able to re-ignite her passion for the game.

Have Fun

It is okay to have fun and not take it all so seriously. Yes, it is important to you, and yes, we all want to win. However, in the end, you must remember it is just a game. An athlete once said that he was so angry at himself after his career ended because he realized that he took it all too seriously and was so nervous about getting minutes or winning his coach's approval that he did not enjoy the process. He realized after going back and playing some pick-up games with his former teammates how much fun it all was. Although the pick-up games were only for fun, the level still was high as he was playing with and against his former teammates. Yet, he played much better because he was able to let his fears go.

All that changed was his mindset. He could have played just as well when he was on the team, but he put too much pressure on himself to be perfect, play like someone else, or impress others. This situation is not unique to this athlete as numerous athletes have told us similar stories after their careers were done. They were so afraid of not pleasing a coach or letting a parent down that they did not play to the best of their ability and they did not enjoy their sport.

Parents, coaches and others will always make comments that make you feel you have to do more or play better. You will always know that scouts want to see you play your best. Although those situations will not change, your mindset can change. Enjoy the challenge by enjoying the game. Have fun running after a 50/50 ball. Take pride in making a diving save. Take pleasure in the pain of the last 50 meters. Appreciate the moments you have playing the sport you love. Some would say your sport career is like a roller-coaster ride. There are ups and downs and sometimes it is even nerve-wracking. However, success is not in just "surviving" the ride, but actually enjoying the process. Next time you feel the challenge is extreme, throw your hands in the air and scream like you would on the downhill of a huge roller-coaster. Push yourself through the moment and just enjoy the ride.

Find What You Enjoy

Take a moment right now to make a list of all of the other aspects of your sport you enjoy that have nothing to do with winning, playing time, coaches, parents or media. What else do you enjoy about being an athlete if you were to take those factors out of the mix? You most likely enjoy being with your teammates, competing in a sport you love, or being active. Focus on these often overlooked aspects of being an athlete so you can find the fun in going to practice every day. In place of dwelling on the negatives, spend your emotional, mental and physical energy in these areas. Focusing on a loss never gets you a win. Complaining about a lack of playing time will not earn you minutes. Focusing on the aspects of the sport you love and working on the areas of the sport you control will, however, increase your enjoyment in the moment. You are more likely to be in a better mood, work harder, and in the end, have a better chance of getting the playing time and performance outcome you desire.

Enjoy All Wins—Even the Ugly Ones

While you most likely strive for it, how often do you actually play a "perfect" game or have a flawless performance? Pat Summitt, the legendary women's basketball coach at the University of Tennessee, says she learned it is important to allow herself and her team to enjoy a win even if it was "ugly." This is important because you probably rarely ever enjoy it when you lose. And if you only enjoy it when you have the perfect performance, then that does not leave too many opportunities to have fun. Although it is not what you strive for, you have to be impressed if you can pull out a win when you are not performing your best.

Similarly, enjoy each competition. We have seen athletes walk away from competitions with barely a smile because they knew they should win. Following the victory, they did not even celebrate. Others are so distraught after a loss they neglect to notice how well they actually performed. As an athlete, enjoy all of the moments. Be proud of accomplishments along the way. If you wait to be happy only after you win the championship, you may be waiting a while and you might lose your passion along the way.

Key Points to Remember

1. Others can only influence your passion for your sport if you let them.

2. See your sport as your sanctuary, your place to escape the outside world.

3. You likely started participating in sport because you loved competing and playing and learning new skills, not because of playing time or winning only.

4. Success is about more than just finishing first.

5. Sport is exciting BECAUSE of the ups and downs, so start enjoying them now.

6. Take a moment to review your answers to the questions at the beginning of the chapter. What changes can you make to help you enjoy the journey more completely?

Conclusion

We started this book by saying we all have a certain level of talent and very few athletes ever maximize the talent they have been given. Too often they are satisfied with being good or too afraid to get better. Jim Collins (2001) discusses the idea that being good at something can be the enemy of being great. This happens to athletes because they become complacent. They get comfortable being good. Others are too scared to take the chance, to put their neck on the line. They are not willing to fail first, so they will never truly succeed. Athletes who become complacent or fear failing either stay where they are or lose ground to those willing to learn more, try new techniques and fail over and over again.

We have attempted to make the argument that great athletes are never comfortable or satisfied with being good because they are confident in their abilities to do better. Do not misinterpret "never comfortable" as meaning "never happy." These athletes enjoy where they are while striving to get ahead. In addition, the great ones give more than lip service to commitment. They actually commit a significant portion of their lives and time to their craft. Much like master craftsmen in other professions take thousands of hours to master their skills, so too must "master athletes." Great athletes have an incredible desire to reach higher levels and they have an unwavering belief in their ability to do so. Great athletes refuse to allow coaches, teammates, media, fans or a few bad performances to shake their confidence or diminish their desire. Great athletes are confident because they know they have trained smarter than their opponents. They look forward to, and embrace, pressure situations. These athletes want to be the "go to player" when the game is on the line. Additionally, the truly great ones demonstrate a high level of character when facing adversity because they also value competing the right way over just winning. These athletes do want to win and they are willing to work very hard to make that happen, but not at the expense of sacrificing their character.

Because these athletes put in the time to train their bodies and their minds, they are more likely to experience those moments in sport we all desire; those moments when everything just feels right. It has been called "being in the zone" or "flow," but it all means the same thing. Athletes strive for those moments when their thoughts are simple, their focus is clear and they feel confident that they can perform effectively. Although these moments are sparse in most athletes' careers, they are possible. So, take the time and practice letting go of mistakes. Use the strategies to help you embrace pressure and act confidently. Take time to employ strategies to make you a mentally tough athlete and over time you will find yourself thinking less, enjoying the moment more and getting closer to being "in the zone."

You might not be as talented as Lance Armstrong, Kobe Bryant, Serena Williams, Peyton Manning or Annika Sorenstam but you have the ability to maximize every ounce of talent you have been given. You can certainly get close to reaching your full potential if you implement the strategies suggested in this book. The focus should be on becoming the best you can be. Set your own goals, define success as much by your attitude and effort as by your skill improvement, and compete in your sport with confidence. Challenge yourself not to be complacent or scared. There are many good athletes out there. Why not separate yourself from the good ones and work to become great? You will look back on your athletic career with pride knowing that you were able to maximize your potential while enjoying the process.

References

Buckingham, M. (2001). *Now, find your strengths.* New York, NY: The Free Press.

Collins, J. (2001). *Good to great: Why some companies make the leap . . . and others don't.* New York, NY: Harper Collins.

Covey, S. (1989). *The 7 habits of highly effective people.* New York, NY: Fireside.

Gough, R. (1997). *Character is everything: Promoting ethical excellence in sports.* Orlando, FL: Harcourt Brace & Company.

Janssen, J. (1999). *Championship team building: What every coach needs to know to develop a motivated, committed and cohesive team.* Tucson, AZ: Winning the Mental Game.

Mack, G. (2001). *Mind gym: An athlete's guide to inner excellence.* New York, NY: McGraw Hill.

Subject and Name Index